Ascent to Excellence

A Blueprint for Healthcare Board and Leadership Success

Teri K. Sholder

ASCENT TO EXCELLENCE

Print ISBN: 979-8-98979-712-7
eBook ISBN: 979-8-98979-713-4

Printed in the United States of America

ABOUT ASCENT TO EXCELLENCE

"Ascent to Excellence: A Blueprint for Healthcare Board and Leadership Success" by Teri Sholder is a groundbreaking guide aiming to enhance health system performance in quality, safety, and efficiency. From transformational leadership to practical tactical approaches, the book offers actionable insights derived from industry knowledge and real-world experiences. Addressing the five key elements outlined in the blueprint brings significant financial benefits to healthcare organizations, including improved revenue streams through data integrity, reduced costs from workforce engagement initiatives, and enhanced operational efficiency through process optimization. The author offers tailored strategies to guide organizations in achieving and sustaining their goals, ultimately saving costs associated with underperformance and missed targets.

Emphasizing board governance and leader commitment, "Ascent to Excellence" provides healthcare leaders with a framework for achieving clinical excellence. The guide concludes with a compelling case study, illustrating a health system's success and serving as a beacon for positive change in an evolving healthcare landscape. Leveraging clinical expertise and leadership acumen, Teri Sholder provides a pragmatic toolkit encompassing concrete strategies, actionable insights, and a holistic, visionary approach to achieving unparalleled clinical excellence.

CONTENTS

FOREWORD

As the former Chair of the Board at BayCare Health System, I am delighted to share my enthusiastic endorsement for our organization's exceptional journey toward becoming one of the top healthcare systems in the nation. Our relentless focus on enhancing quality has not only transformed healthcare delivery across our communities but has also shaped the mindset of the dedicated BayCare workforce. The journey to Clinical Excellence at BayCare reflects the diligent efforts and commitment of the Board of Directors and Chief Executive Officer, who pledged to prioritize quality, safety, and operational efficiency to be our "true north" and not just another key performance indicator. Together, we assembled a capable C-Suite team equipped with the necessary skills and foresight to carefully craft a comprehensive strategic plan that would elevate quality standards and operational efficiency to unprecedented levels.

The Formula for Success

Our success story began with a bold vision: to redefine healthcare excellence. To climb from the bottom quartile in some health system rankings to the top quintile as compared with other U.S. large health systems. At the time, I was serving as Vice Chair of the Board and Chair of Board Quality Committee. We recognized that achieving this goal required more than incremental changes; it demanded a systematic approach that would take some time and the commitment of the entire organization. Thus, we set a timeline to achieve the goal of national top quintile in 5 years. The next step was to fill the vacant Chief Quality Officer position, recognizing the necessity for an experienced leader capable of driving effective change and unifying a workforce of 28,000+ leaders and team members towards a shared objective: Attaining Clinical Excellence.

Teri Sholder joined the organization as the Senior Vice President/Chief Quality Officer under the leadership of Dr. Bruce Flareau, Executive Vice President/Chief Medical Officer. She immediately went to work creating a robust quality improvement framework that everyone in the organization could clearly understand and which ultimately became the cornerstone of our transformational journey.

I succeeded Ray Ferrara as the BayCare Board Chair a little over a year into the five-year Clinical Excellence strategic plan. As I assumed the role of BayCare Board Chair, it became evident that a steadfast commitment to Clinical Excellence was vital for our organization's success. I shared Mr. Ferrara's fervor for delivering the highest quality healthcare to our communities, ensuring a seamless transition in leadership. Our board's engagement was paramount in driving this commitment to excellence.

Board governance serves as the linchpin in ensuring healthcare quality by overseeing and holding healthcare leaders accountable for key performance indicator achievement. While the executive team sets the cultural tone, the board oversees policies and strategic directions that prioritize patient safety, clinical effectiveness, and operational efficiency. Recognizing the significance of our board's dedication to Clinical Excellence, I emphasized the importance of each member understanding the strategic plan's intricacies, metrics, and their impact on our goals. Effective governance hinges on understanding, transparency, ethical decision-making, and a culture of continuous improvement.

Regular meetings outside of formal board meetings with Dr. Flareau, Teri, and myself allowed for in-depth discussions on progress and barriers, ensuring the board could actively support ongoing initiatives. To streamline our understanding, I advocated for standardized board presentations, facilitating "pattern recognition" for myself and fellow members.

Teri's team crafted a graphic illustrating each layer of our bedside to boardroom accountability framework for achieving Clinical Excellence. By incorporating this graphic at the onset of every board meeting, members could visualize their role in this journey. Furthermore, we developed a structured board member introduction to Clinical Excellence, reinforcing the importance of each member's involvement.

We found the keys to effective board governance for quality, safety, and operational efficiency lie in board members:

- Holding themselves and management accountable for performance, quality, and adherence to regulatory requirements.
- Seeking to thoroughly understand the health system strategic plan and ensuring alignment with the organization's mission, vision, values, and goals.
- Election of members with diverse backgrounds and expertise in healthcare, finance, law, and other relevant fields and gaining their commitment to be fully engaged.
- Ensuring transparency by maintaining open communication channels with stakeholders, including patients, team members, and the community.
- Demonstrating a commitment to ongoing education and staying abreast of industry trends, regulations, and best practices.
- Understanding the power of their commitment, engagement, and relentless gratitude to drive organizational success.

Our steadfast pursuit of clinical excellence delivered results and did not go unnoticed. We received accolades from prestigious organizations, including:

- Fortune: Top 100 places to work
- Leapfrog Group: "A" for patient safety for nine of the health system hospitals
- Multiple IBM/Watson 100 top hospitals
- U.S. News and World Report Best Hospitals

Charting the Course: Transformative Journey to Clinical Excellence

As we celebrated our achievements, we remained steadfast in our resolve. Our Quality Improvement Formula is not static; it evolved as we learned, adapted, and innovated. The framework set forth in Teri Sholder's Ascent to Excellence serves as an open invitation for other healthcare boards and leadership teams to embark on this transformative journey. The incorporation of the five elements outlined in Ascent to Excellence proved to be the perfect recipe for our success, providing a comprehensive guide for achieving and surpassing our goals.

In closing, I commend Teri and the BayCare quality team, the dedicated staff, physicians, visionary leaders, fellow board members and supportive community. Together, we elevated healthcare quality and achieved clinical excellence one patient at a time.

Eric Obeck
Chief Commercial Banking Officer
Hancock Whitney Bank

PROLOGUE

While waiting for takeoff on the tarmac, the flutter in my stomach was a combination of excitement and nervousness— both unrelated to the impending flight. I was in route from Ohio to Florida for my new role as the Senior Vice President and Chief Quality Officer at BayCare Health System.

The current performance of the health system at the time fell short of embodying the BayCare Mission and Vision, which aimed to 'set the standard for high-quality compassionate care' and be 'an extraordinary team leading the way to high-quality, personalized, customer-centered health.' The organization had faced challenges in achieving satisfactory results in quality, safety, and operational efficiency, placing it well below average in quality and operational efficiency compared to other large health systems nationally. While a few of the BayCare hospitals were individually ranked above average, the health system's expansion to fifteen hospitals, including the acquisition of lower performing hospitals over the prior decade, negatively impacted its overall national rankings.

BayCare, a not-for-profit health system, had an outstanding Board of Directors. The chair, vice chair and board members were dedicated to the well-being of the communities served and the quality of healthcare delivered by the health system. Meeting with board members was part of my interview process. While this blurred the line between the board's responsibility for governance rather than management, it underscored the organization's unwavering commitment to the quality strategy and goals.

I viewed the board members' participation in my interview as a good sign that this health system leadership team were serious about the quality strategic goals, and I knew this was a critical element in the scope of the journey we were about to embark on.

The objective of my new role was crystal clear. I was to orchestrate a turnaround. To repeat what I had done for another health system and propel BayCare from below average in national performance rankings to the top quintile. The strategic plan outlined a timeline of five years to improve the health system national ranking by over 220%. It was a formidable challenge, but those types of challenges fueled my competitive spirit, and I was ready to get to work. The clock started and now all I needed to do is answer the question...

Where to begin?

INTRODUCTION

> *"We keep moving forward, opening new doors, and doing new things, because we're curious and curiosity keeps leading us down new paths."*
>
> *- Walt Disney*

Career challenges that I hesitantly pursued have given me some of the most valuable lessons in my professional healthcare experience. Those challenges, such as leaving the familiar territory of acute care and exploring other types of healthcare settings have both broadened and enriched my understanding of clinical and operational practices in different healthcare environments.

As an executive with extensive experience in quality strategy for large health systems and post-acute providers, I've observed various approaches to enhancing Key Performance Indicators (KPIs) in healthcare—both effective and ineffective. These experiences have offered valuable insights for developing a successful blueprint to address a wide range of health system improvement opportunities.

To achieve and maintain your organization's objectives, whether in revenue growth, operational effectiveness, or quality improvement, it is crucial to consider key strategic elements that either directly or indirectly impact progress. This involves leadership commitment to rapid and efficient improvement, supported by a comprehensive, long-term strategic plan to enhance overall performance.

Drawing from experience collaborating with outstanding health system boards and leaders, I've formulated a methodology for spearheading significant health system and hospital transformations.

The timeline for achieving success, whether it be a specific goal like reducing length of stay or a broader objective of transforming a health system's strategic plan from vision to results, is contingent upon cultural factors and adaptability to change. The path to improvement begins with the leadership's unwavering commitment to the goal.

Drawing upon five key elements of organizational success, 'Ascent to Excellence' presents a carefully crafted formula aimed at translating a health system's vision into reality. When these elements are nurtured by the health system leaders and integrated into the organizational culture, transformative results become not only attainable but can also manifest at an accelerated pace. This book serves as your compass for instilling a commitment to excellence and adopting a systematic approach that fosters positive and enduring goal achievement.

The experience I've acquired in driving improvement spans different healthcare settings, including large health systems, skilled nursing facilities, home health, and the insurance industry. The ability to pinpoint a process from one health setting, which is impacting outcomes in another setting, is important information for a comprehensive root cause analysis. Acute care length of stay challenges often stem from delays in transitions to post-acute care, attributed to insurance authorizations or inefficient post-acute admission processes.

As I spearheaded care delivery transformation in the acute setting, I knew that gaining insight into operational workflows in the post-acute setting would offer an integrated perspective to fully support overall health system improvement strategies.

This integrated perspective helps refine a formula that not only speeds up improvement but also deals with the unique challenges faced by each organization.

Having a comprehensive understanding of clinical and operational processes in each healthcare setting along a patient's path to recovery provides an ability to seamlessly connect the dots in the care continuum, ensuring safe and effective transitions of care and a positive experience for patients.

Ascent to Excellence takes complex ideas, theories and concepts of organization performance improvement and organizes them into five driving forces and a tangible blueprint for achieving results. By defining expectations, key strategic tactics, and relationships that are relevant to the desired outcome, Ascent to Excellence introduces a systematic approach to move strategic goals from discussions around a white board to sustainable results.

Essential elements of a successful blueprint for driving sustained improvement in many not-for-profit healthcare organizations are already in place. The mission, vision, and value statements of these organizations oftentimes reflect a dedicated commitment to providing high-quality, efficient care to the surrounding communities. As part of regulatory compliance, the Quality Committee of the Board serves as the governing body for the health system's Quality Assessment & Performance Improvement program. If your organization is falling short of its goals or experiencing variability in key performance metrics, crucial components of a clinical excellence framework for driving and sustaining improvement may be missing. This is where 'Ascent to Excellence' steps in to help.

When an improvement opportunity arises, meetings with key stakeholders are planned. Many healthcare leaders waste valuable time and money on ineffective meetings that fail to address the core issues of their organization. Leaders spend hours in recurrent meetings to discuss safety issues or how to reduce readmissions, but when the meeting is over, attendees are distracted by competing priorities. As a result, they only talk about the opportunities, but struggle to find time to act on them.

During a recent annual checkup with my primary care physician, we were discussing quality improvement and goal achievement in healthcare. As a longstanding member of several committees for her affiliated health system, she shared her frustration with the lack of progress toward established goals. Despite dedicating a couple of hours each month to committee meetings, discussions on the same opportunities persist without any tangible results or improvement.

Her opinion is that these meetings, which consume valuable physician and leader time, have become a low-value, high-cost endeavor—deemed by her as nothing short of "a complete waste of my time."

High-quality, safe care delivery, and clinical effectiveness aren't coincidental outcomes. I have worked with leaders who believe these results will naturally emerge by ensuring sufficient staff, adhering to standardized pathways, or establishing additional committees. While these factors may raise awareness of existing issues and potentially influence performance, they fall short of the strategic methodologies employed by the top-performing health systems in the nation.

"Ascent to Excellence" establishes a framework for attaining and sustaining outstanding results, focusing on five fundamental elements: Leadership Commitment, Data Integrity, Workforce Engagement, Process Optimization, and a Culture of Accountability. These elements can take the form of priorities for effective leaders, defining characteristics of productive teams, or benchmarks for high-quality health systems—depending on how they are valued, put into practice, and leveraged. They serve as the foundational components propelling your health system's trajectory to excellence.

As we dive into each element in the upcoming sections, I will provide insights and experiences to assist leaders in overcoming some of the most formidable challenges encountered by health systems striving to achieve and sustain improvement.

ELEMENT 1: LEADERSHIP COMMITMENT

> *"What you do speaks so loudly that I cannot hear what you say."*
>
> *– Ralph Waldo Emerson*

Throughout my professional career, I have been fortunate to collaborate with some of the healthcare industry's most exceptional leaders. These individuals recognized that a thriving healthcare organization relies on the strength of high-performing leaders, held accountable by an engaged and effective Board of Directors. At the core of organizational excellence is leadership commitment to the performance goals, making it the foundational level in "Ascent to Excellence."

The distinction between the standout leaders and their more average counterparts aligns seamlessly with the performance of their respective organizations. High performing leaders do not treat their mission, vision, and values as mere rhetoric on a banner or website. Instead, they translate these principles into a strategic plan with tangible goals. This plan demonstrates genuine support, care, and respect for the community, patients, and workforce, consistently prioritizing the well-being of patients as the foremost objective.

The Storm's Paycheck: Compassionate Leadership and Employee Well-being in the Face of Hurricane Irma's Threat

In 2018, the approach of Hurricane Irma posed a significant threat to an area in Florida that housed one of the state's largest health system hospitals. The hurricane's projected path indicated a direct hit on several of the health system's critical facilities. Faced with the unpredictable potential for Irma's devastation, the health system's leadership took extraordinary measures to highlight their genuine care and concern for their entire workforce and community.

Anticipating the challenges posed by the impending hurricane, the health system's Board and executive team made a remarkable decision. Recognizing that the well-being of their employees was of paramount importance, they issued paychecks a week early. This proactive measure aimed to ensure that each employee had the financial means to secure the essentials needed to prepare for the approaching storm.

This exemplary action during a time of crisis demonstrated, unequivocally, the extent to which the health system's leadership valued, respected, and cared for their workforce. By prioritizing the financial well-being of their employees, the health system's leaders not only set a standard for compassionate and considerate leadership but also confirmed the profound importance of prioritizing people as the organization's most invaluable asset.

Cultivating a Culture of Leader Commitment & System Alignment

A leader's commitment to an improvement goal is an indispensable element in steering an organization towards excellence. When leaders wholeheartedly endorse and actively engage in the pursuit of improvement objectives, it sends a powerful message throughout the organization. This commitment establishes a shared vision and purpose, aligning every member toward a common goal. It transforms improvement from a mere initiative into a core value, shaping the organizational culture to prioritize continuous growth and positive change.

Moreover, leadership commitment and involvement are essential for employee engagement. Employees take cues from their leaders, and when they witness a genuine commitment to improvement, it instills a sense of purpose and motivation. Leaders become not only decision-makers but also role models, inspiring a collective effort to overcome challenges and strive for excellence. This engagement is vital for cultivating a workforce that is not only receptive to change but actively contributes to the innovative solutions necessary for achieving improvement goals.

With leaders dedicated to improvement goals, resources are judiciously allocated and directed, ensuring that the organization has the necessary tools and support structures in place. Additionally, leader commitment enhances organizational adaptability, fostering an environment where challenges are viewed as opportunities for innovation rather than roadblocks. A leader's commitment to improvement goals is the cornerstone of organizational success, shaping the culture, motivating the workforce, and paving the way for sustained positive outcomes.

If your health system aims to operate cohesively rather than as a collection of independently managed hospitals and clinics, the crucial first step is initiating a strategic plan at the system level with shared objectives. Every department's goal within each hospital in the network should align, either directly or indirectly, with the overarching system goals. For instance, if the system's objective for a particular year is to achieve a 4% operating margin, the goals set for all hospitals in the system should align, extending down to individual nursing units, ensuring their objectives have a direct or indirect impact on reaching the system-wide goal of a 4% margin.

During the annual strategic planning process, health system leaders must maintain a clear line of sight to ensure that department goals are coordinated with the system's strategic plan. Furthermore, system-wide goals should be tied to the annual bonuses for both leaders and team members across the health system.

As we move down the organizational hierarchy, goals at the division, department, or nursing unit levels may span different time periods to address specific opportunities that impact the system goal, either directly or indirectly. Goals set across the entire health system enterprise at all levels should consistently align with the health systems strategic plan and be formulated in a structured manner that includes a baseline (X), target (Y) and timeline (when).

Constructing goals in an "X to Y by when" format is a clear and concise way to articulate objectives with a specific target, current state (X), desired state (Y), and a timeline for achievement (by when). This format provides a roadmap that is measurable, and time bound. This goal format offers clarity, allowing for easy tracking and assessment of progress. It can be applied to various contexts, from financial targets and customer satisfaction goals to productivity metrics and quality improvement initiatives.

The framework "X to Y by when" proves its versatility and efficacy in formulating goals that are both actionable and measurable. Boards and leaders should scrutinize goals that omit a baseline or timeframe and should prompt teams to incorporate all three components when defining their objectives.

The Transformative Power of Leadership - A Journey to Shape and Sustain a Positive Healthcare Culture

There are hundreds, even thousands of books on the importance of culture to an organization. Culture is crafted by the norms, behaviors, expectations, and actions of the senior most leader in the company.

A friend and colleague, Jarrod McNaughton assumed the role of CEO for a health plan in California serving over 1.5 million residents (about the population of West Virginia). His vision for the organization's culture went beyond the conventional notions of success. Recognizing the profound impact of leadership on organizational culture, he embarked on a transformative initiative to mold the organization into a beacon of diversity, innovation, empowerment, and accountability.

From the outset, Jarrod understood that culture is not something that just happens; it is something that needs intentional cultivation. Organizational cultures are dynamic. They shift, incrementally and constantly, in response to external and internal changes. He passionately believed that the values and behaviors of the senior leadership set the tone for the entire organization. He began implementing initiatives that would shape a workplace culture where every employee felt valued and inspired.

Diversity and inclusion were not mere buzzwords, they were the cornerstones of Jarrod's vision. He championed diversity, understanding that cultures of organizations are never monolithic and ensuring the organization's workforce was representative of the vibrant communities it served. He actively sought out talent from various backgrounds, fostering an environment where differences were celebrated, not merely tolerated.

Innovation became a rallying cry under Jarrod's leadership. He encouraged a culture where employees felt empowered to think creatively and contribute their ideas. Regular brainstorming sessions, rapid improvement events, and cross-departmental collaborations became the norm. He knew fostering innovation was crucial for staying ahead in the rapidly evolving ecosystem of managed care. And with this focus on innovation, the evolution of the organization began shaping the culture.

Strategic thinking, another pillar of his cultural blueprint, permeated every level of the organization. He encouraged his team to approach challenges with a long-term perspective, aligning their efforts with the organization's overarching goals. This strategic clarity not only improved decision-making but also instilled a sense of purpose among employees.

Empowerment and accountability were intertwined in his leadership philosophy. He believed in giving employees the autonomy to excel in their roles while holding them accountable for their contributions. This balance of trust and responsibility created a culture where individuals felt a keen sense of ownership, leading to increased job satisfaction and performance.

Within five years of Jarrod's transformative leadership, the health plan gained national recognition as one of the top 100 places to work in healthcare. The accolade was not just a reflection of the organization's success on paper but a testament to the positive and inclusive culture that he had carefully crafted. Employee engagement soared, and the health plan boasted one of the lowest turnover rates in the healthcare industry.

Jarrod's journey serves as a compelling illustration of the role effective leadership plays in shaping organizational culture in a healthcare environment. By embodying values such as empathy, diversity, collaboration, and continuous improvement, leaders like him contribute not only to the success of their organizations but also to the well-being of members in the community and the satisfaction of their staff.

Effective leadership is fundamental in shaping and sustaining a positive organizational culture. When leaders like Jarrod embody and promote values that resonate with the workforce and community, these efforts contribute significantly to creating a culture that prioritizes the well-being of people and team member satisfaction.

> ***The essence of leadership commitment lies in the alignment of our decisions with our actions.***

Over the years, I have gained an immense wealth of knowledge about leadership, teamwork, and culture by following the works of Patrick Lencioni, whose literary works and podcasts I admire greatly. His insights on leadership have been particularly enlightening, contributing significantly to my understanding of these crucial aspects. Throughout my career, I have seen how the qualities of Board members, CEOs and the executive teams affect the performance of their organizations.

Value placed on professional leadership growth and development is essential for organizational success. Great leaders build strong relationships and foster a culture of excellence. They lead their organizations to achieve elevated levels of market share, employee engagement, revenue, and quality. Successful organizations do not tolerate poor leadership, because they know that it puts their success at risk.

Through my collaboration with top-performing health systems nationwide, it is evident that a commitment to cultivating exceptional leadership is ingrained at every level. The Board of Directors and CEO/presidents of these organizations recognize the critical role that leadership plays in the success of a health system. They understand that fostering a culture of excellence requires intentional and purposeful initiatives to ensure opportunities for the development of strong leaders.

Health Systems striving to innovate and excel should recognize the value of leadership networking and continuous learning. Leader exposure to diverse perspectives and innovative ideas through conferences and seminars is important for staying ahead in the rapid pace of evolving healthcare science and innovation. Allocating funds for professional leadership development should not be seen as an expense but as an investment in the organization's future.

The intentional strategy of investing in leader growth not only elevates the individual performance but has a cascading effect on the entire organization. The commitment to high standards of behavior and continuous learning fosters a culture of excellence that positively impacts employee satisfaction, patient outcomes, and the overall success of the health system.

Exceptional leadership translates into improved patient outcomes and operational efficiency. Leaders who are well-versed in the latest advancements and best practices are better equipped to guide their teams in delivering high-quality care.

Part I. A Tale of Two Leaders: The Downfall of Mountain Heights Health System

Elliott Johnson, a seasoned executive with a background in healthcare operations, stepped into the role of president at Mountain Heights Health System in Georgia with high hopes. Little did he know that his tenure would be marked by a series of missteps and poor leadership decisions that would ultimately lead to the downfall of the once-promising health system.

Mountain Heights Health System, a three-hospital network, had been acquired by a private equity firm, seeking to capitalize on the lucrative healthcare market. However, despite the financial backing, the system faced numerous challenges, particularly in staffing and workforce engagement, exacerbated by the aftermath of the Covid-19 Public Health Emergency.

Elliott's leadership style, characterized by unrealistic goals and a lack of strategic planning, quickly became apparent. Despite the ongoing staffing challenges and low employee morale, Elliott set ambitious targets for market share growth and profit margins, goals that many within the organization deemed unattainable and disconnected from reality.

The absence of a cohesive strategic plan aligned with the company's mission and vision only worsened the situation. Trust within the organization dwindled, with employees dubbing the system-level administration team "The Capital," a reference to an unfair and uncaring governing body reminiscent of the dystopian world portrayed in the Hunger Games movies.

Staffing issues persisted, with nursing turnover rates steadily climbing. Instead of addressing the root causes of dissatisfaction and disengagement, Elliott and his team adopted a reactive approach, offering incentives such as increased pay and benefits to retain unhappy nurses. This approach not only failed to curb turnover but also created disparities and further discontent among the nursing workforce.

Moreover, the emphasis on financial incentives overshadowed the importance of leadership in driving high performance. Clinical nurse managers found themselves bogged down by administrative tasks, leaving little time for effective leadership and mentorship, further exacerbating the workforce issues.

Elliott's attempt to tie leadership bonuses to goal achievement, including quality metrics and nurse turnover goals, fell short. Unrealistic financial targets meant that bonuses were rarely awarded, further eroding employee morale and engagement.

The true root cause of Mountain Heights Health System's problems lay in its leadership, or lack thereof. While Elliott and the private equity company focused on short-term financial gains, they failed to recognize the critical role of strong leadership in fostering a positive work environment and driving organizational success.

Over three tumultuous years, Mountain Heights Health System continued to hemorrhage customers, grapple with high turnover rates, and fail to establish a positive reputation in the communities it served. Despite numerous attempts to course-correct, the lack of strategic vision and effective leadership ultimately led to the demise of the once-promising health system.

As the dust settled on Mountain Heights Health System's downfall, one thing became abundantly clear: without strategic leadership and a clear vision for the future, even the most well-funded organizations are destined to fail.

Part II. A Tale of Two Leaders: The Rise of Green Valley Health System

In stark contrast to the tumultuous tale of Mountain Heights Health System under Elliott Johnson's leadership, the story of Green Valley Health System and its president, Tom Jenkins, stands as a testament to effective leadership, strategic vision, and unwavering commitment to excellence.

Tom Jenkins, a seasoned healthcare executive with a proven track record of success, assumed the role of president at Green Valley Healthcare with a clear vision and strategic plan for the organization's future. Unlike his predecessor, Tom understood the importance of setting realistic goals aligned with the company's mission and values.

Green Valley Healthcare was a medium sized health system with similar challenges as Mountain Heights Health System. Upon taking the helm, Tom immediately prioritized fostering a culture of trust and collaboration within the organization. Recognizing the critical role of frontline staff in delivering quality patient care, Tom empowered nurses and other healthcare professionals to voice their concerns and contribute to decision-making processes.

Under Tom's leadership, Green Valley Healthcare implemented comprehensive workforce engagement initiatives aimed at addressing employee concerns and boosting morale. Regular feedback sessions, mentorship programs, and professional development opportunities became integral components of the organization's employee retention strategy.

Instead of adopting a reactive approach to staffing challenges, Tom took a proactive stance, investing in recruitment efforts and offering competitive compensation packages to attract and retain top talent. Tom not only addressed staffing challenges but also ensured that existing employees were brought up to industry standards, surpassing or matching the compensation offered to new hires depending on years of service.

Tom and the head of human resources developed a loyalty program, recognizing years of service with recognition and gifts presented at an annual banquet. Recognizing the importance of effective leadership at all levels of the organization, Tom emphasized leadership development programs for clinical managers and executives alike.

Unlike the financially driven mindset of Mountain Heights Health System, Tom understood that sustainable success required a holistic approach that prioritized not only financial metrics but also quality of care, patient satisfaction, and employee well-being. Incentive structures were designed to reward accountability for both financial performance and clinical outcomes, ensuring a balanced focus on all aspects of organizational success. This balanced focus is what creates a framework for organizational financial success.

Tom's strategic leadership and unwavering commitment to excellence bore fruit, as Green Valley Healthcare flourished under his guidance. He realized that a long-term plan required a strategic vision, carefully crafted roadmap, and patience, as turning a good size ship takes time. Employee engagement eventually soared, turnover rates plummeted, and patient satisfaction scores reached new heights. The organization's reputation as a provider of high-quality healthcare services became widely recognized in the communities it served.

Over the years, Green Valley Healthcare continued to thrive, expanding its reach and impact while maintaining a steadfast commitment to its core values. Tom's legacy as a visionary leader and champion of excellence in healthcare was solidified, serving as an inspiration to future generations of healthcare leaders.

Part III. A Tale of Two Leaders: A Leadership Paradox

The narrative of the two leaders highlights the glaring disparity between effective and ineffective leadership within the realm of healthcare. Effective healthcare leaders grasp the fundamental truth that achieving clinical and operational excellence requires more than just ambition—it demands vision, strategy, patience, and a deeply engaged workforce.

In one corner stands the embodiment of poor leadership, characterized by short-sightedness, unrealistic goals, and a lack of strategic direction. This leader fails to recognize the interconnectedness between organizational vision and workforce engagement, leading to a downward spiral of discontent, high turnover rates, and diminished quality of care.

Contrastingly, in the realm of strong leadership, we witness a different narrative unfold—one marked by foresight, strategic planning, and unwavering dedication to organizational excellence. Here, the leader understands that success is not achieved overnight; it is the result of meticulous planning, investment in employee development, and a steadfast commitment to fostering a culture of collaboration, innovation, and accountability.

While these stories are works of fiction, they illustrate the significant influence leadership can have on the trajectory of an organization. While ineffective leadership may lead to stagnation and decline, effective leadership paves the way for growth, resilience, and sustained success despite the volatility in the current healthcare environment.

LEADERSHIP COMMITMENT BUILDING BLOCKS

- [ ] Demonstrate leadership commitment to a priority by aligning incentives with the achievement of goals and allocating resources to establish evidence-based processes that drive the desired results.
- [ ] Translate the hospital or health system mission, vision, and values into tangible goals that prioritize the well-being of the community, patients, and workforce.
- [ ] Model the behaviors you anticipate from your teams. The culture is influenced by the actions and behaviors of senior leaders within the organization, beginning from the highest levels. The way you interact with your teams sets the precedent for how they will interact with their patients and each other.
- [ ] Commit to ensuring the hospital or health system improvement goals resonate with the workforce to establish a shared vision and transform the improvement measure into a core value.
- [ ] Commitment to goals at every level, ranging from system-wide to individual units, must either directly or indirectly correspond with the health system's strategic plan goals, mission, vision, or values.

- ❑ Embrace leadership abilities and expertise while fostering a commitment to ongoing learning and enhancement of qualities essential for exceptional leadership.
- ❑ Champion diversity, embrace and foster innovation, promote strategic thinking, and balance empowerment with accountability to cultivate a positive culture through effective leadership.
- ❑ Assist leaders in recognizing that a long-term strategy comprises short-term tactics, ensuring that the vision remains prominent in the minds of the workforce.
- ❑ Show leadership's dedication to organizational goals by being visible at improvement events and maintaining ongoing awareness of initiatives aimed at goal achievement.

ELEMENT 2: DATA INTEGRITY

> *"Data integrity in healthcare is not a checkbox; it's a commitment to the sanctity of patient information and the cornerstone of quality care."*
>
> *- Teri Sholder*

Data Integrity is an essential component of the performance improvement lifecycle. It is so fundamental that it deserves its own dedicated section in Ascent to Excellence. Linda, the leader of BayCare Health System's Data Analytics team, would often say, "It's all about the data" for every successful improvement initiative. Although there are other elements involved in achieving success, insights from accurate data are crucial to success if you know how to leverage information efficiently and effectively, avoiding the trap of analysis paralysis.

Analysis Paralysis: Simplify Decisions with the 80-20 Rule

Analysis paralysis is defined as the difficulty of making a decision when you have too many options or too much information readily available, causing confusion as to what is relevant and what is not. It can happen when you overthink a problem, worry about the consequences of your choice, or seek perfection in your outcome. Many initiatives get stuck in the data analysis phase because healthcare is a science and clinicians find greater comfort with data analysis as opposed to the next step of having to *act* on the data.

The Pareto principal is the best method for targeting the greatest opportunity for performance improvement. Eliminate time spent on everything and narrow to the top 20% that will solve 80% of the problem. This is a proven method to help leaders get on the right track, focus on the right things, and efficiently work on process improvements. This data analysis method directs focus towards areas with the greatest impact on the goal, preventing wasted time and effort on issues that won't contribute to the desired improvement.

For groups stuck seeking perfection in their solution, this may be a challenging concept, so it is important to realize that the 80-20 rule may not include all variables inherent in the root cause. However, it will capture most of the problems leading to the opportunity and get you on your way to your goal.

Harnessing Data Insights: A Key Driver for Diverse Health System Initiatives

While negotiating a performance-based payment agreement between Anthem Blue Cross and a mid-sized health system in Ohio, the insurer suggested linking payment adjustments to the reduction of hospital length of stay for their members. They aimed to have the system's performance in this area impact a percentage of the annual payment increase. Just a few weeks earlier, I collaborated with another leadership team within the same organization to analyze the reasons behind prolonged hospital stays.

During the assessment, we discovered that 80% of the extended stay issue stemmed from delays in discharging patients to Skilled Nursing Facilities and Home Health Agencies. Further investigation revealed an average delay of 2.9 days, partly attributed to challenges in obtaining authorization from the health system's largest commercial payer, Anthem Blue Cross. This was in line with their interest in tying a portion of the annual payment increase to hospital length of stay. By analyzing the data and pinpointing the 20% of factors responsible for 80% of the hospital's length of stay problem, we identified delays caused, in part, by the insurance company's authorization processes.

Without this thorough analysis, the health system might have entered into a performance-based contract at a significant disadvantage, with delays caused by the insurer leading to unnecessarily long hospital stays for patients.

Data insights can help organizations identify the root cause of their inability to achieve desired goals. By understanding the data available and how it is used across the organization, one can make connections and correlations between the data and organizational objectives. This approach takes the guesswork out of the equation and helps organizations make informed decisions.

Essential Role of Risk Adjusted Data: Impact on Quality, Operations & Billing

If you have collaborated with physicians and their outcomes data, you have likely heard one or more say that the reason their performance is lower than their peers is due to having "sicker" patients to care for. Risk adjustment removes the bias from the data to even the playing field by taking the patients' clinical, demographic, and socioeconomic risk factors into account when calculating observed over expected outcomes.

Risk adjustment is a critical piece to data integrity for outcomes. A patient admitted to the hospital with an acute exacerbation of congestive heart failure can have a wide range of acuity and level of debilitation. Although age is a factor in risk adjustment methodologies, I know 95-year-olds who golf and live independently and would be considered a moderate vs. elevated risk for an adverse outcome. I know 60-year-olds that cannot walk 15 feet without a cane who would have a higher risk level.

Age is only one of many factors calculated in risk adjustment. When assessing performance outcomes, the first question the Board or leader should ask is if the data is risk adjusted. Most health systems rely on external analytics to have their data risk adjusted. There can be up to a 5% difference in raw versus risk-adjusted outcomes.

Risk adjustment is a statistical process that is used to account for differences in patient populations when comparing healthcare outcomes. It involves controlling confounding factors or systematic differences within the defined population of the outcome measure. Confounding factors may be clinical, including diagnosis types, number, or severity of conditions; demographic, which is age and gender, and/or socioeconomic, which includes race, ethnicity, and income. The predominant healthcare risk adjustment methodology in the United States is the 3M APR DRG. This method is employed by the Centers for Medicare and Medicaid Services for generating risk-adjusted publicly reported measures related to quality, safety, and clinical effectiveness.

Examining raw data without adjusting for population risk may result in directing improvement efforts toward what seems like the most substantial opportunity. The absence of risk adjustment makes it difficult to accurately gauge the health system's actual performance.

Healthcare risk-adjusted data is crucial for providing a more accurate assessment of performance, accounting for variations in patient populations. For instance, in analyzing readmission rates, risk adjustment considers factors such as patient age, comorbidities, and socioeconomic status to ensure fair comparisons among healthcare providers. Mortality rates are also subject to risk adjustment, accounting for the severity of patient conditions and other relevant variables.

When examining length of stay metrics, risk adjustment helps normalize data by factoring in the complexity of cases and patient-specific characteristics, ensuring that hospitals are evaluated fairly based on the acuity of their patient population. Similarly, cost metrics benefit from risk adjustment, considering patient complexity and medical conditions to provide a more nuanced understanding of healthcare spending efficiency. By incorporating risk-adjusted data, healthcare organizations can make more informed decisions and implement targeted improvements that enhance overall quality of care.

The Vital Functions of Clinical Documentation Improvement

I was collaborating with an executive team at Grandview Hospital in Dayton, Ohio to assess their quality and efficiency performance in preparation for value-based incentive contracts they were negotiating with their physicians. Two of the hospitalists in the group had considerable opportunity with their risk-adjusted mortality rates. When we were looking into root cause, the leaders said these were great physicians who had large patient panels and a good reputation in the health system. Based on this information, I suspected that it was their documentation or lack thereof that was negatively impacting their quality outcome measures.

Upon further investigation, my suspicions were accurate when we compared these two physician's case mix index with their peers, and the indices were significantly lower. A case mix index (CMI) is a relative value that reflects the diversity, complexity, and severity of a healthcare facility's patients. These two physicians had a very heavy caseload and lacked the time to document appropriately and capture the true acuity of their patients. This led to low outcome scores that made them appear to be poor performing in quality.

In the intricate and ever-changing medical coding environment, precise and thorough clinical documentation is essential for providing high quality, clinically effective patient care. Clinical Documentation Improvement (CDI) plays a crucial role in care delivery, serving as the fundamental basis for diagnosis, treatment planning, decision-making, and reimbursement processes. Furthermore, Clinical Documentation Improvement (CDI) is a fundamental component of modern healthcare management. It not only enhances patient outcomes but also facilitates effective communication among interdisciplinary care teams. Additionally, a CDI program impacts quality improvement initiatives while ensuring financial stability through accurate coding and billing within the healthcare system.

The first documented Clinical Documentation Improvement (CDI) program was developed in reaction to the introduction of the Centers for Medicare and Medicaid Services (CMS) Diagnostic-Related Group (DRG) system for coding and inpatient billing in the early 1980s. However, it was the expansion of the DRG system into Medical Severity - Diagnostic Related Groups (MS-DRGs) in 2007 that brought significant attention within the healthcare industry to the critical importance of capturing specific documentation to accurately portray a patient's true acuity, impacting both revenue and clinical care coordination. The addition of the patient's severity of illness and risk of mortality into the MS-DRG system ensures appropriate reimbursement aligned with the patient's level of acuity.

CDI programs are commonly made up of Registered Nurses who concurrently review the patient records to identify opportunities for greater specificity in the diagnosis. The nurses query the physicians when additional specific or diagnostic documentation appears to be missing. Two key measures in assessing the effectiveness of a CDI program are the percentage of generated queries and the percentage of physician responses which positively impact the integrity of the medical record.

Data integrity & Clinical Documentation Improvement: Because we wouldn't want a patient's diagnosis to transform from 'common cold' to 'yeti attack' during the coding process.

The effectiveness of risk adjustment relies heavily on the physician's adeptness in documenting the acuity of their patients. A precise medical record, characterized by diagnostic specificity, effectively captures the patient's acuity level, offering a distinct and comprehensive overview of individual patients or entire populations. This precision plays a pivotal role in bridging gaps in clinical documentation and care delivery, ultimately ensuring accurate billing and profiling of patient populations.

The assessment and comprehension of data insights pertaining to physician documentation integrity serve as crucial information for health system leaders. In instances of inadequate documentation, it is likely to impact revenue, care delivery, and risk adjustment, creating an impression that the health system manages patients with lower acuity, thus requiring fewer resources.

Evaluating Performance Against Peer Hospitals and Health Systems Using External Benchmark Data

Benchmarking data with external sources will help health systems evaluate their performance against other health systems. The size of the benchmark cohort is important to ensure a large enough volume of data for comparison. If you are a large health system, you want to know how you compare against other large health systems with similar profiles. For health systems or hospitals lacking the ability to invest in analytic platforms to customize benchmark data, an alternative is to use the Centers for Medicare and Medicaid Services (CMS) provider compare sites, however the benchmarks available on CMS Care Compare are national and state averages. This would be manual for analysts to pull, but a suitable alternative if no other risk-adjusted benchmark data is available.

Unleashing the Power of Shared Data on Continuous Improvement

I was presenting to a group of home health nurses at AdventHealth in Orlando on approaches to improve patient and family experience. The agency was not performing well on HHCAHPS (patient satisfaction) and wanted to improve their performance and publicly reported star ratings. As I walked through the various questions on the survey that patients receive to fill out and rate their experience, one of the nurses asked how we knew we were not performing well. I asked the analyst to present the most recent scorecard and was surprised to find out that not one nurse in the room had ever seen a scorecard. They had never laid eyes on the data directly attributed to their work. Once we reviewed the scorecard, they were eager to go back to the survey questions and start working on solutions to improve.

The third discipline in the book "The Four Disciplines of Execution" by Sean Covey, Chris McChesney, and Jim Huling is about creating and sharing a compelling scorecard with teams directly impacting the outcomes. The authors used a football analogy that perfectly represents the consequences of not sharing performance with the teams that produce the data. If football teams did not keep score, how hard would they try to get the ball to the uprights? After sharing the scorecard with the nurses in Florida, the engagement level immediately changed, affirming the importance of team awareness of the outcomes they are directly impacting.

As leaders it is easy to get so wrapped up in the day-to-day meetings and "fires" to extinguish that we don't take the time to discuss performance improvement opportunities or share updated scorecards with our teams. Team members are typically dependent on their leader to share how the organization is performing and, more importantly, how they are contributing to the goals of the organization. Town Halls may provide high level organization performance, but most of the audience is not going to connect their day-to-day work with what the president or executive at the front of the room is presenting.

Most of us have at least a little competitive spirit in us. In my experience, when data is unblinded, shared and compared across health system hospitals, departments and even people, a sense of urgency develops, as no one wants to be in a meeting with peers and be at the bottom of the performance list. It is human nature to be uncomfortable with being in last place. This works well with physicians too but be prepared for excuses from the ones at the bottom of the list. Have your Clinical Documentation Improvement reports ready when they claim their patients are sicker and let them know that if they allege their patients are sicker, their clinical documentation is not supporting their claims.

Cultivating Openness and Resilience in Performance Reporting

The fear of sharing data that reflects inferior performance in front of peers, other leaders, or Board members can stem from numerous factors, and in addition to experience, overcoming this fear requires a combination of self-awareness, a positive organizational culture, and strategic communication. When we discuss a cadence of accountability in a later chapter, you may want to bookmark this page to refer to the fears and solutions below.

A cadence of accountability is built on transparent reporting of performance at all levels of the organization. The apprehension leaders' experience below are much higher for those with limited experience sharing performance with an audience, regardless of the audience size or composition. Presenting is a nerve-racking proposition for most people. Presenting poor performance can be terrifying.

Leaders often experience a fear of judgment, driven by concerns about being perceived as ineffective if data exposes shortcomings in their area of responsibility. Additionally, a natural human fear is a tendency to worry about what others think of us and this can create hesitancy in sharing data whether it reflects negatively or positively.

I vividly remember my first experience as a nurse manager delivering quality performance reports to a Board of Directors. The executive responsible for this task was out of town, and as I stepped into their shoes, my nerves took over, causing my voice to shake along with my legs. I stumbled through the meeting, unable to answer some of the board's questions coherently. It was a humbling experience, and the hospital president, Roy Chew, who would later become my boss, offered invaluable advice: "Say what you know, know what you say, and if asked, be totally transparent about what you don't know."

His encouragement to embrace imperfection and acknowledge uncertainties became a guiding principle. He assured me that each stumble was an opportunity to gain experience and grow, recognizing that overcoming challenges would better prepare me for the next encounter with the board. This leadership approach fostered resilience and development by allowing me to navigate speaking challenges and emerge stronger.

Creating a conducive learning culture involves encouraging a growth mindset and emphasizing the value of improvement over perfection. Trust is essential, and leaders should focus on building trustworthy relationships within the team to foster collaboration. Shifting the focus from blame to problem-solving, leaders should present not only data but also strategies for improvement, demonstrating a commitment to positive change.

Transparent communication, including open acknowledgment of challenges, builds credibility and shows leadership's awareness and dedication to improvement. Leaders should exemplify accountability by admitting mistakes and committing to rectifying issues, setting a precedent for others.

Leaders who can create an environment where sharing data, even when it reflects poor performance, is seen as an opportunity for growth and improvement are more likely to overcome the fear associated with it. By fostering a culture of continuous learning and improvement, leaders can turn challenging situations into catalysts for positive change.

DATA INTEGRITY BUILDING BLOCKS

- ❑ Acknowledge the fundamental role of data integrity in the performance improvement lifecycle.
- ❑ Combat analysis paralysis by applying the Pareto Principle (80/20 rule) to target the most impactful opportunities for improvement.
- ❑ Demonstrate the significance of data analysis in strategic decision-making, particularly in negotiations or performance-based contracts.
- ❑ Recognize the importance of risk adjustment in removing biases from outcomes data.
- ❑ Monitor Clinical Documentation Improvement performance at the executive level to ensure on-going documentation integrity.
- ❑ Utilize benchmarking data from external sources to evaluate and compare organizational performance.
- ❑ Promote a transparent culture by disseminating the organization's performance data in comparison to its goals to individuals across all levels of the organization.
- ❑ Ensure improvement efforts are reflected in a process-focused approach.
- ❑ Encourage a growth mindset, emphasizing the value of improvement over perfection.

- ❑ Benchmark data against an external peer cohort to accurately gauge performance compared to similar organizations.
- ❑ Every leader should be required to report performance data to an audience that encompasses individuals in higher positions within the organization.

ELEMENT 3: WORKFORCE ENGAGEMENT

> *"A true leader has the confidence to stand alone, the courage to make tough decisions, and the compassion to listen to the needs of others."*
>
> *- Douglas MacArthur*

In the early 2000s, Kettering Medical Center's executive team in Dayton, Ohio, sought improvement and engaged with Quint Studer's consulting company after being inspired by his book, "Hardwiring Excellence." Studer's innovative approach to enhancing overall organizational performance presented an appealing opportunity for Kettering leaders, offering a solution to drive improvements across key performance indicators.

To implement Studer's principles, the Kettering executive team devised five strategic pillars: People, Service, Finance, Quality, and Growth. Each pillar had goals of equal weight, linked to potential monetary bonuses for both leaders and employees.

For the People pillar, Kettering established two measures—patient satisfaction and employee engagement. At the time, it didn't occur to me that tying employee engagement to all employees rather than just leadership bonuses could create a perverse incentive for employees to inflate their engagement scores beyond what they might have otherwise. This realization emphasizes the importance of carefully designing and implementing strategies to foster genuine workforce engagement, ensuring alignment with broader organizational goals and values.

As part of this framework, the People pillar emerged as a critical foundation, emphasizing the significance of employee engagement alongside patient satisfaction.

A decade prior to joining the Kettering executive team, I assumed my first leadership role as a nurse quality manager. After a few months in my new role, it was time for the annual employee engagement survey. I was excited to hear the positive accolades from my team and confidently assumed my team would rank high in overall engagement. I could not wait to get the results.

Reviewing the actual engagement results was an eye opener. Reading the comments was painful. After all, I had an open-door policy and made earnest efforts to make sure they liked me. I thought I was doing everything right as a leader. The problem was that I did not know what the right thing was. I may have been nice, but nice was nowhere near enough and almost irrelevant as it related to employee engagement.

Understanding and addressing employee engagement requires more than a manager's likability. The realization that employee surveys reflect broader engagement strategies rather than personal affability is a key insight I learned quickly over the years that followed. Simply having an open-door policy and striving for likability is not sufficient.

True engagement stems from strategic approaches such as providing clear communication, fostering a positive work culture, offering professional development opportunities, recognizing, and rewarding achievements, ensuring fair and transparent policies, and promoting a sense of purpose and accountability within the organization. High performing employees will leave if low performing employees are tolerated. In a culture of accountability, leaders ensure their teams are responsible, and teams hold each other accountable. Such an environment highlights low performers, making their performance disparities more noticeable.

The ability to discern the significance of working in an organization with a highly engaged workforce and working in one with low engagement may not have been possible had I not experienced the cultural difference between time spent in healthcare organizations with prominent levels of engagement and those with low levels of employee engagement.

This book does not go into the correlation studies between employee engagement and nursing turnover. However, based on my personal experience, high performing organizations have had lower nurse turnover rates than those healthcare organizations that continuously struggled with quality, engagement, and financial performance.

The key to fostering nurse engagement and loyalty towards an organization and its leaders lies in ensuring that engagement strategies align with the values and priorities of the diverse generations comprising the workforce. Among the shared priorities across generations are professional development, work-life balance, and recognition. However, notable differences exist, particularly between Baby Boomers and subsequent generations like Millennials and Gen Xers. Millennials and Gen Xers prioritize open communication and transparency, challenging traditional organizational practices such as keeping pay information confidential, a practice rooted in Baby Boomer culture. The need for secrecy around pay seems illogical to Millennials, who value fairness over secrecy.

Additionally, integrating innovative clinician roles can enhance nurse satisfaction and retention. Traditionally, moving nurses away from bedside roles may have been met with resistance, but adopting hybrid roles where nurses split their time between bedside care and other organizational functions can address both professional development needs and the retention of essential resources at the bedside. By understanding and accommodating the diverse values and needs of nurses across generations, organizations can create environments that foster engagement and loyalty among their nursing staff.

The foundation of the nurse-patient relationship lies in trust, respect, caring, compassion, and empathy. When these values extend beyond bedside care and become ingrained in the organizational culture at all levels, nurses experience a profound sense of being understood, valued, appreciated, and accepted. This recognition does not imply that nurses should receive preferential treatment over other disciplines or that undesirable behaviors should be tolerated. In fact, when these high standards of behavior are combined with an established culture of accountability, the organization has the perfect ingredients to foster nurse engagement.

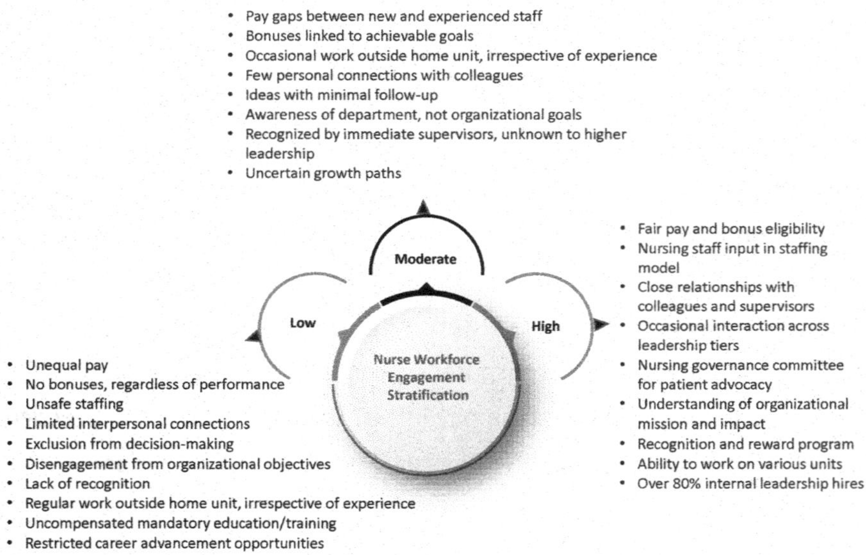

Whatever Happened to "Hire for Cultural Fit"?

One word: COVID. I recently sat in the Emergency Department of a hospital with my brother, who has early degenerative dementia in addition to a host of chronic conditions. The emergency department was part of a hospital I was very familiar with due to not only having worked there in the past, but also having spent a lot of time there with other family members over the years. As a leader of healthcare quality and patient experience, I purposefully try and see the care delivery and environment through the lens of the "customer" every chance I get and since my brother's acute condition was not critical, this opportunity was no exception.

Throughout 2014 and into 2015, I was in this same emergency room several times with my mother for a range of reasons. Back then, I remember how impressed I was by the pristine environment – extremely clean and shiny floors, neat and tidy placement of the patient care equipment, the professionalism of the staff. The genuine caring attitudes of the nurses, radiology technicians and physicians were consistent at each visit. Once she was admitted to the nursing unit, she received the same level of genuine care and concern for her well-being.

When confronted with staffing shortages and overburdened existing staff managing high patient loads, the pressure to fill vacancies quickly can lead to compromising on hiring standards. In the face of a worsening nursing shortage, the temptation to hire individuals who may lack the necessary personality traits or clinical skills becomes all too real. These candidates, who may not have been considered under normal circumstances due to poor cultural fit or performance, may find themselves hired out of necessity. Unfortunately, their presence can have detrimental effects on the workplace environment.

These "low performers" may exhibit negative behaviors that are tolerated due to the critical need for nurses. Their presence can be likened to an infection, spreading negativity and eroding morale among their colleagues. The dissatisfaction of high performers is particularly affected, as they witness the impact of these individuals on the overall team dynamic. The adage "one bad apple spoils the bunch" resonates strongly with those who have experienced the consequences of poor hiring decisions. In such challenging times, it becomes imperative for healthcare organizations to carefully balance the urgency of filling positions with the importance of maintaining standards and preserving workplace culture.

Nursing Shortage: Beyond the Band-Aids

In the wake of the Covid-19 Public Health Emergency (PHE), healthcare witnessed a seismic shift, exacerbating deep-rooted issues within a pre-existing nursing shortage that has consistently trended upward over the last two decades. Seated in my brother's examination room, I couldn't help but overhear the discontent brewing at the nurses' station nearby. Conversations brimmed with complaints about staffing shortages, rival hospitals offering sign-on bonuses, and the perceived advantages of travel nursing, often punctuated by expletives.

The atmosphere felt discordant, a far cry from the professional and caring environment I remembered from past visits. Basic needs went unmet, and critical details slipped through the cracks as nurses struggled under the strain of understaffing and burnout. The experience reinforced my concern that monetary incentives alone were insufficient to address the underlying issues driving the nursing shortage.

Consider the case of Brian, an ICU nurse with over three decades of experience. Despite his invaluable contributions and sterling reputation, Brian found himself forced to work outside his specialty due to staffing shortages. Faced with the prospect of sacrificing quality care for the sake of filling gaps, Brian made the difficult decision to retire early—a casualty of decisions made in response to the nursing shortage exacerbated by the pandemic.

Across the nation, hospitals scramble to attract and retain nursing talent, offering eye-watering sign-on bonuses and competitive wages. Yet, these financial incentives, while effective in recruitment, often fall short in fostering a sustainable and cohesive workforce. The influx of contract nurses, commanding premium rates, further strain team dynamics and jeopardize care continuity.

The allure of sign-on bonuses creates a rift between transient staff and those who remain committed to their hospitals, sowing seeds of discontent and eroding team morale. Moreover, the reliance on contract staff has the potential to compromise quality of care and produce a culture of uncertainty and instability.

As hospitals grapple with the repercussions of the nursing shortage, some resort to drastic measures, such as shutting down nursing units or curtailing surgery volumes—a stark reminder of the urgent need for a more holistic approach to workforce management.

The nursing shortage transcends mere numbers—it represents a crisis of engagement, morale, and organizational culture. To address this multifaceted challenge, healthcare leaders must prioritize creating environments where nurses feel valued, supported, and empowered. Laughter should echo in the break rooms, friendships should flourish, and a sense of purpose should pervade every interaction.

When I think back on my days as a staff nurse, some of my fondest memories coincide with moments of laughter and camaraderie with my co-workers. Our nursing team was widely regarded as one of the hospital's finest, known for delivering exceptional care to our patients. We approached our responsibilities with dedication and seriousness, when necessary, yet we also embraced opportunities for fun and companionship. Never did I wake up dreading a shift; instead, I looked forward to the bond we shared and the mutual commitment to both our patients and each other.

Within our unit's subculture, respect for others, care, and mutual support were deeply ingrained, and our pursuit of high-quality care was never compromised by the joy and laughter we shared. To this day, I remain friends with the nurses and physicians on that unit.

While financial incentives may offer temporary relief, the enduring solution lies in fostering workplaces where nurses not only survive but thrive. These environments are characterized by trust, respect, accountability, and the ability to laugh and enjoy the company of peers, providing a foundation for nurses to navigate the emotional demands inherent in their profession. Although these elements may address some aspects of the nursing shortage, they alone may not resolve its complexities. However, by prioritizing such strategies, we can chart a course toward a more sustainable future for nursing engagement and retention.

Addressing the nursing shortage necessitates a multifaceted approach that goes beyond simply hiring more nurses. One crucial aspect of this strategy involves eliminating non-value-added tasks for nurses. These tasks, such as duplicate documentation and redundant administrative duties, consume precious time and detract from the core responsibilities of patient care. By streamlining processes and optimizing workflows, healthcare organizations can significantly reduce the burden on nursing staff, allowing them to focus more on direct patient care.

Duplicate documentation is a common issue in healthcare settings, where nurses often find themselves entering the same information multiple times into different systems or forms. This redundant documentation not only wastes time but also increases the risk of errors and inconsistencies in patient records. By enhancing electronic health record (EHR) systems with interoperability features, healthcare organizations can minimize duplicate documentation by ensuring that information entered once is automatically shared across all relevant platforms.

Nurses: masters of the keyboard, champions of copy-paste, and connoisseurs of documenting the same intervention in ten different places.

In addition to addressing duplicate documentation, healthcare organizations can focus on process optimization to improve efficiency and reduce the demand on nursing time. This involves identifying and eliminating inefficiencies in workflows, such as unnecessary steps in medication administration or patient transfer processes. By streamlining these workflows and implementing standardized protocols, healthcare organizations can maximize the time and resources available to nursing staff, allowing them to devote more attention to patient care.

Overall, eliminating non-value-added tasks and focusing on process optimization are essential long-term strategies for addressing the nursing shortage and improving patient care outcomes. By reducing administrative burdens and increasing efficiency, healthcare organizations can empower nurses to work more effectively and efficiently, ultimately leading to better outcomes for both patients and healthcare providers.

Leadership Impact: Nurturing Culture and Employee Engagement

Measuring organizational culture is not a complex task; it can be gauged through the health system's performance on Key Performance Indicators (KPIs). Drawing on my experience as an executive leader who has witnessed various health system cultures and their impact on organizational performance, I have compiled a list of defining characteristics. These characteristics are grouped into cultural attributes observed in excellent, complacent, and toxic environments. While these attributes may cross category boundaries, each cultural type exhibits distinguishable characteristics. Notably, parallels emerge between the culture types and aspects of the health system's quality, operational efficiency, and financial performance.

Characteristic	Excellent Healthcare Culture	Complacent Healthcare Culture	Toxic Healthcare Culture
Leadership	Collaborative and Inspirational Leadership	Laissez-faire or Micromanaging Leadership	Authoritarian or Unsupportive Leadership
Communication	Open and Transparent Communication	Limited or Selective Communication	Poor Communication or Lack of Information Flow
Teamwork	Strong Team Collaboration and Mutual Support	Lack of Collaboration and Individualism	Hostile or Competitive Environment
Accountability	Emphasis on Accountability and Responsibility	Lack of Accountability or Blame Culture	Blame-Shifting and Lack of Individual Ownership
Innovation	Encourages Innovation and Continuous Improvement	Resistance to Change or Status Quo	Stifles Innovation and Creativity
Patient-Centered Focus	Prioritizes Patient Care and Satisfaction	Focus on Routine or Process over Patient Needs	Neglects Patient Well-being or Satisfaction

Learning Culture	Embraces Continuous Learning and Professional Development	Resistant to Training or Skill Enhancement	Hostile to Learning and Development Initiatives
Work-Life Balance	Promotes Work-Life Balance and Staff Well-being	Ignores Work-Life Balance or Overworks Staff	Disregards Staff Well-being and Burnout
Ethical Standards	Strong Commitment to Ethical Standards and Integrity	Ethical Complacency or Ambiguity	Disregard for Ethical Standards or Unethical Practices
Feedback and Recognition	Regular Feedback and Recognition for Achievements	Lack of Recognition or Inconsistent Feedback	Negative or Unconstructive Feedback
Diversity and Inclusion	Values Diversity and Promotes Inclusive Practices	Lack of Diversity or Inclusive Initiatives	Discriminatory Practices or Exclusionary Culture
Employee Empowerment	Empowers Employees and Encourages Autonomy	Micromanagement or Lack of Empowerment	Disempowers and Undermines Employee Autonomy

While recognizing that organizational culture is dynamic and contains many subcultures, categorizations can serve as a useful tool for leaders to assess and address cultural factors potentially driving or inhibiting success within their respective health systems. It is important to view these categories with flexibility and an awareness that no model of cultural categorization is precise, and nuances exist based on the unique conditions of the organization. To gauge where your health systems culture falls on the category spectrum, I encourage you to take the culture assessment at the end of the book.

In any organization, leaders bear a significant responsibility in fostering employee engagement. Creating an atmosphere characterized by respect, trust, and care should permeate from the organization's top echelons down to the front lines. It is a universal desire—employees at every level seek the same elements. Executives, just like frontline staff, yearn to feel valued, respected by their superiors, form connections with colleagues, and receive acknowledgment for their contributions.

These essential factors for satisfaction should be integrated throughout the entire organization, reaching beyond frontline teams. Boards extend these elements to their CEOs, and CEOs, in turn, provide them for their executives, creating a cohesive and engaged workforce. The resulting positive culture not only enhances retention but also nurtures a sense of joy and fulfillment, laying the foundation for achieving aspirational goals.

I gained profound insights into impactful employee engagement strategies through collaboration with Brenda Kuhn, PHD, RN when she served as Chief Nursing Officer for Kettering Health System. As an adept leader specializing in the recruitment, training, and retention of an engaged nursing workforce, Brenda displayed a remarkable understanding of the human spirit and the sacred work of nursing. She led with genuine care and compassion while simultaneously upholding a culture of accountability within her team.

She recognized and cultivated the fundamental human desire for appreciation and ingeniously transformed it into a comprehensive four-part nursing engagement strategy. The first tactic involved the thoughtful expression of gratitude through personalized Thank You Notes to front line teams, recognizing their exceptional contributions that positively impacted patient care. These notes went beyond generic appreciation, recognizing specific instances where team members exhibited extraordinary dedication or implemented innovative solutions, fostering a culture of acknowledgment and encouragement within the organization.

Receiving a personalized note from a senior leader, especially for a staff member who rarely interacts with them or may never have interacted, signifies a profound acknowledgment. It communicates, "*We know your name and you are special to us; We see the value you bring to our patients and our organization. You are appreciated.*" These genuine expressions of gratitude go beyond simple appreciation; they foster a sense of collective dedication to providing exceptional healthcare experiences. Furthermore, the impact extends beyond the individual, as families of staff members have conveyed their gratitude to leaders for the meaningful recognition, highlighting the significance of such gestures in uplifting spirits and strengthening bonds within the healthcare community.

The next approach entailed purposeful rounds on units to foster meaningful connections with frontline teams. Leaders were obligated to allocate time for discussions regarding the team's achievements and obstacles. This approach generated valuable insights, which leaders documented, allowing for the reinforcement of positive aspects and swift resolution of any concerns or issues raised by team members. While unit rounds by leaders are a well-known practice, Brenda ensured that these interactions were meaningful, documented by her leaders, and that challenges expressed by the teams were promptly addressed.

The third, aptly named "Walk in my Shoes," required active participation from the CEO and executive team. They dedicated regular hours to shadowing employees, gaining invaluable firsthand insights into both successes and challenges. Post-shadowing, executives collaboratively engaged in debrief sessions, addressing barriers, acknowledging individual efforts, and reinforcing positive aspects highlighted by employees.

As the fourth part of the strategy, Brenda established interim nurse engagement targets for each nursing director. Equipping them with tools and training, she implemented scheduled "pulse" surveys where a random subset of nurses from each director's team were surveyed to assess the progress in improving engagement. The nursing directors were given clear engagement goals and held accountable for achieving engagement milestones.

Remarkably, the health system not only met but exceeded its employee engagement goals, propelling employee satisfaction to the top quartile the following year. A noteworthy outcome was the substantial improvement in nursing turnover, a significant metric that witnessed a marked decrease compared to previous years. This success demonstrated

Brenda's exceptional ability to blend empathy and accountability, fostering an environment where employees felt valued and supported.

Fostering a collaborative culture through 360° feedback

The integration of behavior standards into annual evaluations, coupled with the adoption of a "360° evaluation," represents a best practice approach that yields significant benefits in enhancing overall employee engagement. Unlike traditional supervisor-to-employee evaluations, the 360° evaluation is a comprehensive method that involves collecting feedback from various sources, including peers, subordinates, and leaders.

The key advantages of this innovative approach include:

- ❑ Holistic Performance Assessment: By gathering insights from different perspectives within the organization, a 360° evaluation offers a more holistic and well-rounded view of an employee's performance. This comprehensive assessment goes beyond the supervisor's viewpoint, providing a richer understanding of the individual's contributions and areas for improvement.
- ❑ Increased Accuracy and Objectivity: The inclusion of feedback from multiple sources reduces the risk of bias and subjectivity that may be present in a single-supervisor evaluation. This approach promotes fairness and accuracy in evaluating an employee's strengths and areas that need development.
- ❑ Identifying Blind Spots: Peers and subordinates often observe aspects of an employee's performance that may not be immediately apparent to supervisors. A 360° evaluation helps in uncovering blind spots, allowing for a more thorough identification of skills, behaviors, or competencies that may impact overall engagement.

- Enhanced Self-Awareness: Employees receiving feedback from various sources gain a deeper understanding of their strengths and areas for improvement. This increased self-awareness can contribute to personal and professional growth, fostering a sense of ownership and commitment to continuous development.
- Team Collaboration and Communication: The process of seeking feedback from peers and subordinates fosters a culture of open communication and collaboration within teams. This, in turn, can positively impact overall team dynamics and contribute to a more engaged and cohesive work environment.
- Tailored Development Plans: With a comprehensive understanding of an employee's performance, supervisors can create more targeted and effective development plans. This personalized approach supports employees in reaching their full potential, aligning their goals with those of the organization.

The integration of behavior standards into annual evaluations, particularly through the implementation of a 360° evaluation, is a best practice that promotes a more thorough and collaborative assessment of employee performance. This approach contributes significantly to fostering a comprehensive employee assessment through the lens of their supervisors, peers, and subordinates.

The Heart of Engagement: Nurturing Relationships

Engagement is enhanced when nurses feel trusted, respected, and appreciated for their contribution. I've had discussions with many nurse friends who have spent much of their career working on the same nursing unit or Intensive Care Unit of a hospital. Every one of them attributes their longevity to physicians who respect and trust them, leaders that hold them and their co-workers accountable, and relationships that extend beyond great teamwork on the nursing unit, to genuine interest in each other's lives outside of work.

I have nurse friends who cherish the thank-you notes they receive from leaders as special keepsakes. They say the genuine recognition and feeling appreciated by their leaders is one of the reasons they love their job. It does not take high pay or material rewards to drive engagement. Engagement takes fair and equitable pay, a safe staffing model, recognition from leaders, trust and respect from physicians and camaraderie with co-workers.

Team building exercises do not build teams or magically create teamwork. These exercises may show the individuals the value of teamwork, but the seed to great teamwork dynamic is the team relationships that cross the professional boundary into meaningful, caring friendships. These relationships cannot be formed from games played in a conference room. Getting away from the pressures and stress of work and getting to know each other as people forms personal bonds that can blossom into strong teamwork on the unit.

In the early years of my nursing career, I joined the night shift in a surgical intensive care unit known for its exceptional teamwork and rare open positions due to low nursing turnover. The clinicians on the unit, some with over a decade of service, shared a loyalty that extended beyond the hospital—they were friends. There was a fundamental trust and respect nurtured among physicians and nurses. Years later, upon returning to town for the funeral of a nurse from that unit, the close connections within the nursing team still existed. A few of the nurses continued to stay connected beyond retirement. I observed a mournful yet comforting reunion of nurses who had worked together almost two decades prior. This special moment highlighted a team that epitomized teamwork, respect, and loyalty to each other and the patients they served.

This cohesive unit was under the leadership of a manager who understood how to drive workforce engagement. Setting lofty expectations, involving the team in hiring decisions, and cultivating a culture of accountability, trust, and respect were key aspects of her leadership. The nursing unit leader made sure staffing was adequate, respect was a core value and everyone on the team had the tools to do their jobs effectively. This created an environment that enabled bonds to be formed into friendships and teamwork that made the unit the most sought-after place to work in the hospital.

The experience at the funeral service was a touching reminder of the intricate nature of employee engagement. It accentuated the importance of addressing a broader spectrum of leadership attributes which drive and sustain employee engagement, contributing to the creation of a thriving and motivated workforce.

The team's success was not a mere result of casual interactions; rather, it stemmed from a deliberate commitment to behavior standards, hiring practices emphasizing cultural fit, and consistent leadership modeling of trust, respect, and appreciation. While not a simple approach, it proved instrumental in creating a workplace where nurses, physicians and other staff who worked on the nursing unit felt valued, connected, and engaged.

WORKFORCE ENGAGEMENT BUILDING BLOCKS

- ❑ Invest in strengthening front-line leadership skills.
- ❑ Highlight the importance of your personnel as the organization's most valuable asset by regularly allocating time to engage with physicians and staff, understanding their roles, acknowledging successes, and addressing challenges.
- ❑ To engage teams in organization goals, ensure the performance achievement baseline, target and timeline are clear and tied directly to bonuses for leaders and employees.
- ❑ Recognize the significant impact of employee engagement on retention, patient satisfaction, and the quality of care.
- ❑ Understand the cultural difference between organizations with high and low levels of engagement.
- ❑ Evaluate your health system core values for alignment with trust, respect, caring, compassion, and empathy, all of which should extend to organizational behavior expectations.
- ❑ Develop an atmosphere of camaraderie and teamwork by creating environments where expectations are clear, respect, care and compassion are the rule and team members hold themselves and their peers accountable for behaviors and actions.

- [ ] Implement 360° evaluations to foster a comprehensive process that enhances employee engagement.
- [ ] Reward loyalty through events planned to highlight employees years of service
- [ ] Send Thank You notes that include hand-written genuine appreciation for specific contributions vs pre-printed notes.
- [ ] Actively round on your teams, getting to know their names, their families' names, and try to discover what you and they may have in common – a favorite football team, ice hockey, movies, etc.

ELEMENT 4: PROCESS OPTIMIZATION

> *"The secret of change is to focus all of your energy, not on fighting the old, but on building the new."*
>
> *- Socrates*

Over the years spent learning the intricacies of driving organization performance, I recognized that clinical leaders may perceive performance improvement solely through the lens of presenting outcomes data. In meetings, performance metrics were displayed, but there was an apparent void thereafter. Through the remainder of these meetings, I was anticipating a discussion on the root causes behind the metrics falling short of goals and the necessary process changes. Unfortunately, this crucial aspect of the improvement process was consistently overlooked.

This ineffective method of achieving and sustaining goals relies on the belief that looking at data will change behavior and outcomes will improve. I have seen this approach repeatedly and I have seen it fail every time. Poor and/or variable outcomes are the by-product of poor and/or variable processes. When reviewing performance data that is not achieving the desired outcomes, leaders should look for the process changes that are occurring to change the outcome and ensure a direct correlation. Process improvement plans must be measurable to be impactful. Anecdotal improvement goals are ineffective.

As I led improvement efforts over the years, it became apparent that emphasizing the distinction between process measures and outcome measures was an essential part of educating leaders and teams on tactics to achieve goals. An evidence-based process-oriented approach involves implementing interventions that can be directly influenced in real-time.

Inconsistencies in the implementation of evidence-based processes, depending on the individual conducting the interventions, will result in variable outcomes. Prioritizing the reduction of variability through adherence to evidence-based processes, influenced entirely by the individual and their promptness in administering the procedures, will inevitably have a positive impact on the desired outcome. This emphasizes the paramount importance of process optimization in steering toward desired outcomes.

Healthcare Artificial Intelligence (AI) Solutions: Unleashing the Potential

The healthcare industry is experiencing a surge in the availability of AI solutions designed to improve healthcare quality, safety, and efficiency. These solutions encompass diagnostic tools, predictive analytics, natural language processing, and more. The incorporation of AI-driven healthcare solutions holds the promise of eventually transforming health system operations and clinical care, surpassing human capabilities in terms of efficiency and accuracy, but there is a need to address the concerns healthcare leaders have expressed regarding privacy, automation bias and concern over the impact on current provider practice. As innovative data analytic solutions advance, quality improvement tools become more refined, enabling rapid process optimization for enhancing efficiency, improving patient outcomes, and ensuring the sustainable delivery of high-quality care.

I recently participated in a rapid cycle improvement event designed to uncover inefficient utilization management processes and establish clear criteria for transitioning patients from acute to post-acute care in a Skilled

Nursing Facility (SNF). I could not help but see the process of determining medical necessity for SNF admission reduced from an RN reviewing records to assess for appropriate level of post-acute care, to AI technology that not only determines medical necessity, but can distinguish between different payor criteria with the information delivered in nanoseconds.

Process optimization without requiring human intervention has the potential to create unprecedented efficiencies in healthcare. Although it is not a popular thought among the people who do this work, AI could do a sizable portion of case manager, social worker, managed care authorization and claims department functions. As AI continues to evolve, it is important for the health system board of trustees and senior leaders to understand AI's ability to make informed decisions that could help reduce costs by improving operational efficiency, automating administrative tasks, predicting outcomes, and personalizing the plan of care. AI technologies require stringent regulatory oversight to safeguard operations, patient privacy protection and patient safety. As AI gains popularity in health systems, leaders will need to develop policies and guidelines that address these concerns and to ensure AI is used in a responsible and ethical manner.

Streamlining Healthcare Workflows: Navigating Challenges for Process Optimization

> ***Who needs efficiency when you can have a healthcare process that rivals a labyrinth? We've got more twists and turns than a soap opera, but hey, we eventually get there...we think!***

Process optimization in healthcare begins with a meticulous examination of existing workflows to identify bottlenecks, redundancies, and areas of inefficiency. This necessitates the involvement of teams in a transparent and engaged manner as they dissect the workflows. When events, such as Rapid Cycle Improvement process mapping, are organized to uncover these inefficiencies, there is often an underlying apprehension among individuals who may be affected by the identification of wasteful work.

"Process creep" occurs when obstacles are addressed by adding additional processes and steps to achieve tasks. When the right things are not done upstream, the downstream create work-around processes and over time these downstream additional processes become embedded in job descriptions, standard operating procedures, and interdepartmental transactions. Over time the department staffing is aligned with the volume of work, and the productivity standard is seemingly aligned with the work that needs to be done. Process impairment becomes the norm. This is why it becomes difficult for leaders and teams to "see" that they have opportunity for process optimization.

Over time, these workarounds accumulate and become standard procedures. As process mapping reveals inefficiencies and efforts are made to streamline work, the reduction of non-value-added tasks may pose a risk to certain jobs. This response is not uncommon, even in a well-cultivated environment with a foundation of trust and strong leadership.

Achieving efficient process optimization in healthcare necessitates allowing healthcare professionals to invest time, consideration, and effort in the process change, including a thorough examination of all potential implications arising from the new workflow. Although streamlining work and establishing effective processes offer apparent benefits, leaders often find it challenging to allocate sufficient time to this endeavor. Beyond implementing sound change management strategies, leading operational change requires involvement from stakeholders, and engagement from senior leaders to ensure ongoing commitment to the new process. Frequently, improvement projects encounter delays after opportunities are identified, as executing process change demands a substantial effort.

The Old Ways: Regulatory Compliance and Quality Assurance

Process optimization goes hand-in-hand with ensuring regulatory compliance and maintaining high-quality care. By establishing robust processes that align with industry regulations, healthcare organizations not only mitigate risks but also enhance the overall quality and safety of patient care.

Leaders should grasp the distinction between Quality Assurance and Quality Improvement, with the latter being a more proactive and prevalent approach in modern healthcare. In the early 1970s, before the advent of advanced models in healthcare quality improvement, quality was primarily associated with regulatory compliance. This involved a reactive process of auditing and subsequently correcting processes or procedures that deviated from established standards.

While Quality Assurance has a role in healthcare, it should primarily serve as a distinct focus for Regulatory Compliance teams ensuring corporate compliance and adherence to regulatory standards in patient care rather than driving performance improvement. Achieving goals such as reducing readmissions requires a proactive approach focused on performance improvement, a distinctly different approach from auditing records for regulatory compliance.

The history of quality assurance and proactive quality improvement has evolved significantly, with notable developments during the Industrial Revolution and a shift towards proactive approaches in more recent times. My friends and former work colleagues, who are certified experts in performance improvement, would express disappointment if I did not seize this opportunity to highlight the significance of the surge in quality improvement models that align seamlessly with achieving sustainable and high-quality healthcare outcomes.

During the Industrial Revolution (18th to 19th centuries), the focus was primarily on mass production and efficiency. The assembly line and mechanized processes led to increased production, but the emphasis on quality was often lacking. Products were frequently inconsistent, and defects were common. The prevailing mindset was to inspect and sort out defective items *after* production, rather than preventing defects in the first place.

After World War II, particularly in Japan, there was a change in basic assumptions with the introduction of Total Quality Management (TQM) principles. Figures like W. Edwards Deming and Joseph M. Juran played key roles in promoting statistical methods for quality control. This represented a shift from quality assurance, which involves inspecting products reactively for defects, to quality improvement, which entails proactively enhancing the processes responsible for a desired outcome.

In the latter part of the 20th century, Lean Manufacturing and Six Sigma methodologies came to the forefront. Lean concentrated on pinpointing non-value-added tasks and eliminating waste to enhance efficiency, while Six Sigma aimed to minimize defects and variations in processes. These approaches became essential components of quality improvement initiatives in healthcare.

In recent decades, there has been a shift towards proactive quality improvement. Rather than solely relying on inspections and corrective actions, organizations emphasize preventing defects and improving processes before issues arise. Continuous improvement methodologies, such as Kaizen, encourage a culture of ongoing refinement.

Today, process optimization and quality improvement in healthcare demand an integrated approach involving key stakeholders to transparently reveal barriers and defects in processes. Organizations are progressively embracing agile methodologies, integrating quality improvement throughout the entire development spectrum, beyond defined quality measures, and recognizing its broader application to health system operations.

Strategic Insights for Healthcare Process Optimization: Navigating Behavioral Change

Process optimization in healthcare requires a strategic approach, an open mind, and an objective perspective. Identifying inefficiencies, leveraging technology, prioritizing patient-centric care, optimizing resource allocation, embracing data-driven decision-making, and maintaining compliance allow healthcare organizations to navigate operational complexities more efficiently, thereby elevating the standard of care. Achieving process optimization necessitates behavioral change, a complex process that requires a carefully constructed approach. Understanding individuals involved, acknowledging the need to change, and using tools and methodologies rooted in cognitive science for sustainable and effective change is crucial but challenging.

There is a distinct difference between the time it takes to implement what I refer to as stroke of the pen decisions vs. process optimization that requires behavioral change. "Stroke of the Pen" actions can lead to improvements which take little time and require minimal to no behavioral change. Pay raises, approving a new analytic tool or replacing an employee that retired are examples of stroke of the pen actions.

The time it will take for a health system to achieve a desired improvement is based on many variables, including the scope of the goal, current performance and the size of the hospital or health system. However, a pathway to accelerated results is paved when the health system board and executive team set a strategic goal with a realistic timeline and provide leaders with the tools and support to make it happen.

Many health systems have wisely invested in Performance Improvement teams. Performance Improvement Specialists typically have a degree in business, science, or engineering. The best Performance Improvement team I worked with were all mechanical engineers and six sigma black belts with certification in Lean processing. Terms like A3 thinking, Lean processing, Six Sigma Black Belt and Plan Do Check Act (PDCA) are familiar to the ears of health care professionals, but the true value of these improvement concepts is often lost because their deliverables are steeped in driving sustained behavior change, which takes time, patience, and a culture of accountability.

Process optimization commences with a comprehensive exploration to identify the root cause of improvement opportunities and formulate effective solutions, including an implementation plan. This is a critical juncture where leaders may grow impatient or competing priorities might push the execution of a process improvement to the back burner. The positive outcomes of excellent improvement initiatives frequently manifest only when behaviors are altered to firmly integrate the process change and propel improvement. Although the performance improvement team lays the groundwork for improvement, leaders must play an active role in both executing and monitoring the impact of the change.

"Most leaders would agree that they'd be better off having an average strategy with superb execution than a superb strategy with poor execution." - Sean Covey. Co-Author, The Four Disciplines of Execution.

In performance improvement circles, it is widely known that a large majority of improvement initiatives fail at the execution phase. I quoted the contributing author Sean Covey because his "Four Disciplines of Execution" (4DX) has been my framework to ensure successful execution of improvement initiatives for most of my career. By following the disciplines and learning how to steer around roadblocks, I have championed teams that have been able to successfully execute transformational change that led to sustained high quality and operational efficiency.

Over the years, I have suggested the 4 Disciplines of Execution (4DX) to many colleagues, peers, physicians, and team members. If you are acquainted with the book, you will identify intermittent strands of practical wisdom derived from the 4DX methodology. More crucially, having undergone the results of adhering to the 4DX framework, I have seen improvement initiatives progress from planning and strategizing to navigating the intricate facets of execution and producing desired results.

PROCESS OPTIMIZATION BUILDING BLOCKS

- ❑ Shift the focus of performance improvement in healthcare organizations from presenting outcomes data to actively identifying and addressing root causes and necessary process changes for enhanced effectiveness.
- ❑ Choose a proactive quality improvement strategy over manual quality auditing, emphasizing the significance of optimizing processes for sustainable and high-quality healthcare outcomes.
- ❑ Embrace the potential of AI solutions in healthcare to transform operations and personalize patient care. However, prioritize addressing concerns related to privacy and automation bias for responsible implementation.
- ❑ Prioritize superb execution during the implementation phase of improvement initiatives, recognizing that outstanding execution is crucial even with an average strategy.
- ❑ Direct healthcare leaders to regularly assess for efficiency opportunities related to process creep, addressing embedded workarounds and non-value-added processes over time.

- ❑ Stress the importance of a process-oriented approach in healthcare, distinguishing between process measures and outcome measures to effectively achieve desired outcomes.
- ❑ Acknowledge and allow sufficient time for behavioral change, recognizing it as an essential component for achieving lasting process optimization in healthcare.
- ❑ Routine process mapping of workflows can unveil inefficiencies and the elimination of non-value-added activity leading to time savings and operational efficiency.

ELEMENT 5: CULTURE OF ACCOUNTABILITY

> *"Culture outperforms strategy every time; and culture with strategy is unbeatable."*
>
> *- Quint Studer*

For as long as I can remember, I have consistently held myself accountable for my actions, the repercussions of my decisions, and the goals within my realm of responsibility. I believe that possessing self-accountability is an important trait for leaders at all levels, and as one ascends the leadership hierarchy, the importance of this trait becomes increasingly critical.

Accountability is by far one of the most important attributes you will recognize in successful healthcare organizations. Self-accountability is also a trait you will recognize in all high performing leaders and employees. While "accountability" and "responsibility" may share some similarities in meaning, they are distinct concepts. Responsibility is focused on tasks and is associated with specific duties or roles, reflecting the obligation to fulfill assigned tasks within a well-defined scope. On the contrary, accountability goes beyond mere task completion and role fulfillment. It underscores the broader impact of actions, emphasizing the obligation to take responsibility for the outcomes and consequences of one's actions.

Recognizing that the alternative terms suggested for accountability, such as "responsible person," "champion," or "sponsor" fell short in comparison to assigning accountability to an individual, I have persisted in promoting the use of "Accountability" and assigning it to an individual rather than a group. The essence being, when accountability is distributed among multiple individuals, it tends to dissipate, leaving no one truly responsible.

Several years back, during an executive team meeting at BayCare Health System, we were going over the tactics outlined in the health system's strategic plan. A new leader on the executive team was presenting his approach to enhance delivery times in a region where surgeons had voiced concerns about delays in receiving surgical supplies. In an attempt to attribute the delays to his director in that region, the new leader unwittingly placed blame on a specific leader on his team.

Those of us familiar with the CEO, Tommy Inzina, concealed our amusement, anticipating the CEO's response. Seizing the moment, the CEO queried the new leader, "Whose neck do I choke when the next surgeon calls me to complain about surgery delays due to a lack of surgical supplies?" After a nervous pause and a fleeting search for rescue, the new leader admitted, "Mine." The CEO simply responded with a nod, acknowledging it as a satisfactory answer. Mr. Inzina's question was obviously not literal, but it effectively made the point, that from his perspective, in the cadence of accountability, the executive over Supply Chain was solely accountable for outcomes within his division.

Cultivating Accountability: Navigating Organizational Dynamics and Strategic Alignment

> ***"We've got a 'blame it on the ghost' policy here: if something goes wrong, it's probably just the department poltergeist up to their old tricks again".***

A culture of blame and a culture of accountability represent starkly contrasting organizational dynamics. In a blame culture, the emphasis is on assigning fault and pointing fingers when challenges arise. This environment breeds fear of repercussions, stifles communication, and inhibits creativity and problem-solving. It often results in a fragmented and siloed workforce, where individuals distance themselves from collective goals.

On the other hand, a culture of accountability fosters transparency, responsibility, and a proactive approach to addressing issues. In this culture, individuals are encouraged to take ownership of their actions and contribute collaboratively to solutions. It creates an atmosphere where mistakes are viewed as opportunities for learning and improvement rather than as grounds for punishment. A culture of accountability is characterized by shared responsibility, open communication, and a collective commitment to achieving organizational goals.

Frequently, the health system strategic plan originates in the C-Suite and may clash with the prevailing cultural attitudes, beliefs, and behaviors ingrained in the organization's fabric. While having a robust strategy is crucial for goal achievement, if the organizational culture diverges from the strategic direction, the strategy is bound to fall short of realizing the envisioned outcomes.

When leaders of a performance improvement initiative find themselves requiring the "buy-in" of individuals or groups for the initiative to advance or thrive, it indicates a potential issue of misaligned goals among higher-level leaders or a breakdown in effectively communicating clear goals throughout the organization. However, when improvement initiatives align with the organization's strategic goals, the concept of "buy-in" becomes obsolete, as it is replaced by fostering participation and engagement in collective efforts to achieve a shared objective.

Leadership alignment, particularly at the executive level, is paramount to achieving organizational goals and ensuring the delivery of high-quality patient care. Healthcare leaders, whether at the helm of boards, hospitals, clinics, or large healthcare systems, play an important role in steering their organizations toward success. Health system leaders are role models of behavior for their teams, and this includes how they hold themselves accountable for their scope of responsibility.

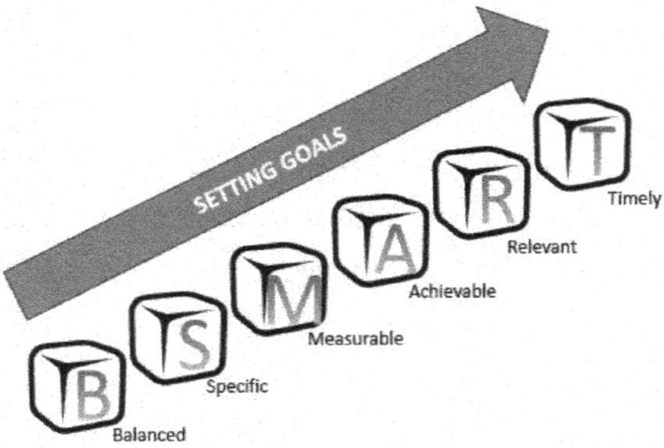

To steer healthcare organizations toward success, CEOs must articulate a compelling strategic vision that aligns with the mission of delivering exceptional patient care, improving outcomes, and meeting the evolving needs of the community. Achieving this vision necessitates the formulation of strategic goals that are "BSMART"—**B**alanced, **S**pecific, **M**easurable, **A**chievable, **R**elevant, and **T**imely. By incorporating the concept of "Balanced" within the existing SMART goal framework, emphasis is placed on achieving equilibrium across key performance indicators (KPIs) in critical areas such as quality, patient satisfaction, employee engagement, financial outcomes, and growth. This comprehensive strategic approach ensures that the objectives are not only aligned with the overarching vision of a thriving and sustainable health system but also encompass the diverse elements that drive overall organizational success and viability.

Simplicity in Goals: Cultivating Accountability Across Healthcare Organizations

When it comes to goals, less is more. By setting one or two clearly defined goals, a health system can adopt a more focused approach towards driving improvement efforts. Different hospital divisions and service lines may have their own goals to address unique opportunities, but their priority should be goals that align with the overall objectives of the organization and contribute to its success.

When the goals of each division and service line align with the overall objectives of the health system, accountability permeates every level of the organizational hierarchy. Leaders should cultivate a culture ingrained with accountability, achieved by establishing clear performance expectations, instilling a sense of responsibility among team members, and acknowledging and rewarding accomplishments.

It is imperative to transparently communicate organizational goals to all stakeholders, including healthcare professionals, staff, and patients, extending beyond one-time emails or town hall slides. Frequent dissemination of the health system's vision and goals throughout the organization ensures that each department, including the physician medical staff, comprehends its contribution to the overarching objectives, fostering a shared commitment to common goals.

Effective leaders go beyond merely setting goals; they actively take ownership in crafting, executing, monitoring progress, and adjusting the strategic roadmap to ensure success. Exceptional leaders extend the expectation of ownership to their direct reports, fostering a unified and aligned team.

Embracing Accountability: Integrating Authority, Compassion, and Respect in Leadership Culture

A culture of accountability is paramount for realizing the organization's vision and achieving desired results. Effective accountability entails granting individuals decision-making authority over tactical approaches and process-level interventions. This authority empowers them to align decisions with the health system's overarching goals, fostering a natural incentive to contribute positively to desired outcomes. With decision-making authority, individuals can respond swiftly to challenges, make timely adjustments, and navigate unforeseen circumstances, crucial for achieving outcomes within specified timeframes.

The integration of decision-making authority ensures a cohesive strategy in line with the health system's direction. This alignment establishes a clear line of responsibility, promoting a sense of ownership and encouraging decisions with a keen awareness of their impact. This coherence extends to resource allocation, allowing for efficient deployment and optimal results.

Authority and Accountability on a bedrock of Compassion, Courtesy & Respect

In fostering a culture of accountability within an organization, the virtues of leader compassion, courtesy, and respect play a crucial role in shaping a positive and constructive environment. These qualities are not only essential for maintaining a healthy workplace atmosphere but also serve as vital components in achieving accountability without generating negative perceptions.

Leaders who embody compassion, courtesy, and respect create a foundation of trust and open communication. When individuals feel valued and respected, they are more likely to embrace accountability willingly, viewing it as a constructive element rather than a punitive measure. This positive approach contributes to a culture where individuals are motivated to meet their goals and responsibilities.

Moreover, the combination of compassion, courtesy, and respect with accountability enables leaders to navigate challenges with a human-centric approach. If a leader identifies that an individual is struggling to meet goals, or if the individual's skills may be better suited for a different role, a compassionate leader can engage in a dialogue rather than resorting to blame or punishment. This allows for a more nuanced understanding of the situation, potentially leading to a solution that benefits both the individual and the organization.

By incorporating compassion, courtesy, and respect into the accountability framework, leaders can foster an environment where individuals are not afraid to admit challenges or ask for help. This, in turn, facilitates a more proactive and collaborative approach to problem-solving, ensuring that organizational goals are met with a sense of collective responsibility.

Leaders possessing compassion, courtesy, and respect are integral in creating a positive accountability culture. By embracing these qualities, leaders not only mitigate negative perceptions associated with accountability but also create an atmosphere where individuals can thrive, and adjustments can be made thoughtfully for the overall benefit of both individuals and the organization.

Leadership accountability is the linchpin for achieving strategic goals and ensuring the delivery of exceptional patient care. Effective healthcare leaders set the vision, establish clear and measurable goals, and foster a culture of accountability throughout their organizations. By actively embracing a leadership model of accountability aligned with authority, compassion and a caring demeanor, leaders are equipped to drive and sustain transformative change and goal achievement.

CULTURE OF ACCOUNTABILITY BUILDING BLOCKS

- ❑ Demonstrate accountability in your own actions.
- ❑ Clearly outline the roles, responsibilities, and expectations for each team member, promoting clarity and accountability within the team.
- ❑ Ensure that individual goals of team members are in harmony with the broader organizational objectives, fostering alignment and accountability.
- ❑ Provide appropriate resources and tools necessary for concentrating on priority improvement initiatives, facilitating focused efforts and accountability.
- ❑ Acknowledge that health system strategic plans may encounter challenges when conflicting with established organizational culture, highlighting the need for aligning cultural values with strategic goals.
- ❑ Communicate organizational goals transparently, promoting understanding and commitment at all levels of the organization, fostering a shared sense of accountability.
- ❑ Ensure that decision-making authority is closely tied to accountability, enabling prompt responses, efficient resource deployment, and adaptability essential in the healthcare environment.

- ❑ Emphasize the importance of compassion, courtesy, and respect alongside authority and accountability, cultivating a workplace culture based on trust and positivity.
- ❑ Establish a mechanism to monitor and track performance improvement across all organizational levels.

ELEMENTS IN ACTION

BayCare Health System:
A Transformational Journey Case Study

I assumed the role of Chief Quality Officer at BayCare Health System in West Central Florida, entrusted to lead the organization's quality improvement strategy. Prior to joining BayCare, a national report was published by IBM/Watson, ranking the health system in the bottom quartile of the nation when compared to other large health systems overall performance. The board, in conjunction with the president, responded proactively to this performance ranking. They established the organization's strategic plan with a clear objective: to achieve clinical excellence, as measured by reaching the national top quintile within the next five years.

As healthcare continues to evolve at an extremely rapid pace through advances in science and technology, achieving and sustaining clinical excellence requires a strategic approach that encompasses a deliberate elemental framework. When the elements of the framework become woven into the organizational structure, they drive overall performance towards unparalleled success. The BayCare case study outlines how each of the five elements in "Ascent to Excellence" led to the successful transformation of care quality and clinical effectiveness across the health system. However, the same elements are relevant to a wide range of KPI opportunities, from focus on a single improvement metric, such as readmission reduction to broader initiatives like overall health system improvements.

Quality Philosophy

The health system had a long-standing Quality Philosophy of "Customer Needs," "Process Focus" and "Continuous Improvement." The philosophy served as guiding principles to foster a data-driven, process focused approach to performance improvement based on research and evidence-based practice. The components of the philosophy were captured in a graphic model of quality in the form of a triangle that connects steps in the quality process of Planning, Improving, Assessing and Reporting supported by the Quality Philosophy and encircled by key promoters of culture: Leadership, Education & Training, Communication and Recognition and Reward.

Although the Quality Model served as an excellent guide for enhancing performance improvement efforts, the health system lacked a distinct strategic direction and goals to unite organizational leaders toward a shared objective.

Variable performance across the health system hospitals reflected a lack of coordination, standardization, and consistency among the systems hospitals, ambulatory centers, and home health agencies. In an abbreviated period, the distinct vision of Clinical Excellence and an overall system goal with clearly defined measures aligned the hospitals and other divisions of the organization toward a shared objective, fostering an environment of collaboration, connections, and seamless care continuity across the various health system settings.

The board of directors and senior leadership team established an unwavering dedication to Clinical Excellence, setting clear objectives that sparked a renewed enthusiasm for performance improvement across the entire organization. The pursuit of clinical excellence resonated with physicians, leaders, and team members at all levels within the health system.

The bedrock of any successful organization is unwavering leadership commitment. Leaders who ardently champion a commitment to excellence set the tone for the entire organization. Their dedication, visible through actions and decisions, establishes a culture that prioritizes patient care, safety, and continuous improvement. This formula places a strong emphasis on leadership dedication, encouraging a steadfast and exemplary approach. By setting the right tone at the top, we can craft cascading values that foster a culture that is both inspiring and motivational.

Governing the quality of healthcare involves understanding specific metrics, goals, and the benchmarks used for comparison. Eric Obeck, the chair of the BayCare Quality Committee and subsequently appointed Chair of the Board possessed ideal leadership qualities. His business acumen and passion for community care were pivotal in the transformation experience.

The Health System Board of Directors, comprised of carefully selected members who were pillars in their surrounding communities, demonstrated openness and engagement in learning to govern healthcare quality programs. Some members, including physicians and local business leaders, were initially less familiar with healthcare Quality Assessment and Performance Improvement (QAPI) but actively participated in the learning process. To facilitate this, we initiated a Board of Directors introduction to Health System QAPI governance, fostering an environment conducive to learning and understanding the intricacies of the health system's quality program. Additionally, we articulated a clear vision of Clinical Excellence and the roadmap to Top Quintile performance.

When I joined the organization, the hospitals measured outcomes using a ratio called "observed over expected" (O/E), with a goal set at an O/E ratio of 1.0. This ratio considers factors like the severity of illness to predict the likelihood of adverse outcomes. Achieving an O/E ratio of 1.0 means the hospital is performing as expected.

In the previous year, despite meeting the set goal, some of the hospitals received suboptimal safety grades from a national ranking organization. The confusion arose from not aligning the goal with an external benchmark. For reference, the benchmark for top quartile performance in complications of care, based on the IBM/Watson 100 top hospitals report, was an O/E ratio of 0.74.

Unfortunately, the health system leaders unintentionally set goals at a level that aimed for mediocrity, resulting in just that. The positive aspect is that most of them had some type of goal achievement framework. The setback, however, was in setting aspirations too conservatively.

Ascent to Excellence: The Strategic Vision

The Board unanimously recognized that achieving Clinical Excellence requires a comprehensive set of metrics, encompassing operational and financial measures to govern the overall health system performance effectively. Although the metrics in the national report used for percentile rankings may change periodically, the measures listed below consistently contribute to determining the annual overall performance ranking for large health systems. These specific measures were selected by the board and the executive team due to their reflection of a comprehensive evaluation of clinical excellence and effectiveness.

Influence Beyond Hospitals

While the yearly published rankings incorporate hospital-based performance, various settings within the health system significantly impact performance on many measures. This includes the health system's surgical centers, home health agencies, and primary care.

1. Mortality: Risk-adjusted rates for medical conditions and surgical procedures.
2. Complications: Risk-adjusted complications of care, including surgical complications.

3. 30-Day Hospital Readmissions: Risk-adjusted readmission rates for medical conditions and surgical procedures.
4. Patient Experience: Results from the Hospital Consumer Assessment of Healthcare Providers and Systems (HCAHPS) survey.
5. Hospital-Acquired Infections: Infections acquired during hospitalization.
6. Emergency Department Measures: Median time patients spent in the emergency department before hospital admission.
7. 30-Day Mortality: Mortality for specific conditions within 30 days of hospital discharge.
8. Severity Adjusted Average Length of Stay
9. Medicare Spend per Beneficiary: Healthcare costs 3 days prior to the index hospital admission through 30 days post-discharge.

These measures collectively defined the health system's standing in the national report, showcasing a comprehensive evaluation of its overall clinical performance. A delay in data publication prompted the data analytics team to create a scorecard closely mirroring the report calculations, enabling the estimation of percentile rankings and progress tracking.

Quintile Goals and Transparency

The objectives for each measure aimed for a top quintile ranking when compared to other large health system quality measures. To ensure measurement equity among hospital presidents, each hospital shared the same measures, with the top quintile goal benchmarked against hospitals of comparable size.

The Clinical Excellence scorecard, developed by the exceptional data analytics team, displayed system performance in each measure. The scorecard, color-coded to reflect threshold, target, and stretch performance, set goals at prior-year performance, top quintile, and top decile, respectively. Recognizing the importance of transparency, I collaborated with the analytics team to expand the scorecard's drill-down capability, allowing visibility into hospital and nursing unit performance.

Enhancing Visibility for Improvement

The drillable scorecard aimed to guarantee alignment and concentration on health system goals for clinical excellence. Further improvements included the ability to drill down to the top three opportunity drivers for most measures. This enhanced functionality pinpointed units with the greatest improvement opportunities, enabling hospital leaders to identify areas in need of improvement and prioritize efforts promptly. This initiative alleviated "analysis paralysis" by providing immediate access to primary opportunities influencing goal achievement.

In the age of big data, harnessing information is crucial. Data-driven insights empower healthcare leaders to make well-informed decisions. The capacity to rapidly analyze patient outcomes, operational efficiency, and other vital metrics, along with the capability to pinpoint specific areas for improvement, accelerates the process of performance improvement. By leveraging data, we gain a deeper understanding of our organization's overall health status, enabling us to make efficient strategic choices that drive positive outcomes.

Ensuring Data Insights and Integrity

Further initiatives to guarantee comprehensive data insights and data integrity involved an evaluation of the health system's Clinical Documentation Improvement (CDI) program. The accuracy of risk-adjusted clinical outcomes data hinges entirely on the quality of physician documentation in the medical record. Given the unprecedented level of specificity now required for accurate coding in the healthcare industry, a robust CDI program is indispensable. The emergence of CDI programs in the mid-2000s was prompted by the introduction of new billing codes that mandated specific language in the medical record to precisely capture the patient's condition and acuity.

Many of the health system Clinical Excellence goals were risk-adjusted outcomes. Readmissions, Mortality and Length of Stay are examples of risk-adjusted or severity adjusted outcomes that, when calculated, are influenced by the acuity of the patient population as reflected in the physician documentation. The Clinical Documentation Improvement (CDI) team within the health system operated with half the necessary staff according to industry standards for an institution of its size.

Comprising of registered nurses, the CDI team was expanded to industry standards of productivity and consistently delivered a commendable 4 to 1 return on investment by upholding the integrity of medical record documentation and ensuring precise coding. This accuracy is essential for enabling precise risk adjustment, directly influencing the "expected" figure in the Observed/Expected (O/E) ratio. Failing to capture accurate risk adjustment may result in patients appearing less ill in the data than their actual health status warrants.

With the expansion and implementation of a strong CDI program and assurance in the integrity of clinical documentation throughout the health system, there were no longer worries about the risk-adjustment process accurately capturing patient acuity in the data analytics.

Linking Performance Bonus to Clinical Excellence

The health system adhered to a standard annual bonus structure applicable to all levels of leadership and team members, with the percentage contingent on the position's placement in the organizational hierarchy. The performance bonus was linked to three key performance domains. Service, measured by employee and physician engagement, Quality Outcomes, comprised of a composite of the nine Clinical Excellence goals, and Cost, gauged by Operating Margin.

Recognizing Clinical Excellence as the paramount priority of the health system, the BayCare executive leadership team believed that the weighting of each bonus-linked goal should align with this organizational emphasis. Accordingly, Clinical Excellence was given double the weight of the other two domains. This bonus structure was another way the organization showed commitment to prioritizing clinical excellence, reinforcing their stance that Clinical Excellence and effectiveness stood as the foremost goal of the health system.

From Evaluation to Engagement: Cultivating Core Values for a Thriving and Engaged Healthcare Culture

The core values of an organization should reflect ideal behaviors and attributes that are prioritized and embedded in the culture. BayCare's core values include trust, respect, and a commitment to excellence—standards of behavior that resonate with most people, especially clinicians. To ensure that these values translate into standards of behavior, they were incorporated into the annual comprehensive employee evaluation. During this process, subordinates, peers, and superiors provided an assessment of the employee's performance. The behavior standard assessment was a part of every team member evaluation, including the CEO of the health system as assessed by the Board of Directors.

An Engaged Workforce is the lifeblood of clinical excellence. Motivated and satisfied healthcare professionals contribute to a positive patient experience and improved clinical outcomes. A positive correlation between high employee engagement and high patient satisfaction is a subject of many research studies. Fostering a culture that encourages employee engagement, professional development, and open communication creates a collaborative environment where healthcare teams can thrive.

Prioritizing Workforce Engagement by tying it to leader bonus compensation, acknowledges the pivotal role employees play in goal achievement and reinforces that people are the organization's most treasured asset. A motivated team fosters innovation, collaboration, and a collective commitment to organizational success.

When employees understand how their work contributes to the organization's outcomes, they feel a sense of pride in themselves and the health system they work for. This sense of pride is not just about a paycheck, a thank you letter, or bonus pay. It is about being a part of something bigger than themselves. By involving team members in improvement efforts that lead to desired results and the achievement of organizational goals, team members contribute to the success of the organization and feel a sense of accomplishment. This is a key ingredient to a highly engaged workforce.

Physician Engagement in Clinical Excellence

Dr. Bruce Flareau, the Executive Vice President, and Chief Medical Officer of the health system at that time, was renowned for his multiple published works on physician engagement and health system leadership. He garnered widespread recognition and respect from the organization's employed physician group and the Board of Directors. Working closely with Dr. Flareau, Bill Ulbricht, President of the BayCare Physicians Medical Group, played a crucial role in implementing the tactics outlined in the health system's strategic roadmap. Together, they ensured that health system physicians were actively engaged and aligned with the Clinical Excellence strategy.

The achievement and surpassing of physician engagement goals significantly contributed to the overarching pursuit of organizational clinical excellence. A concerted effort was made to enhance physician engagement through a multifaceted approach, including monthly rounds on several physician offices by each member of the executive team. The objective was to demonstrate support and appreciation for contributions to the health system mission and vision and to identify any concerns that could be addressed.

The success of physician engagement initiatives can be attributed to several key factors developed and implemented by Dr. Flareau and Bill Ulbricht. They prioritized channels of open communication, fostering transparent dialogue between leadership and physicians. This facilitated a shared understanding of organizational goals, enabling physicians to actively contribute their expertise towards achieving Clinical Excellence.

Recognizing the importance of involving physicians in decision-making processes, Bill Ulbricht established mechanisms for their meaningful participation in shaping policies and protocols. This instilled a sense of ownership among physicians and leveraged their frontline insights to continually refine clinical practices.

Moreover, Dr. Flareau managed the health system's investment in ongoing professional development opportunities tailored to physicians' evolving needs. By providing access to the latest medical advancements, training programs, and continuous learning, he empowered physicians to stay at the forefront of their fields and demonstrated a commitment to their growth and success.

The significance of physician engagement in the pursuit of organizational Clinical Excellence cannot be overstated. Engaged physicians are more likely to exhibit higher levels of commitment, dedication, and collaboration, resulting in improved patient care, streamlined clinical workflows, and the implementation of evidence-based practices.

By year four into the Clinical Excellence journey, physician engagement at BayCare Health System reached the top 15% in the country. The health system's commitment to physician engagement and surpassing goals played a crucial role in the journey to Clinical Excellence. Recognizing physicians as integral partners in this pursuit fostered trust in the administration team, leading to higher engagement and greater involvement in health system improvement initiatives.

Foundations of Process Optimization

Process Optimization is crucial to streamlining operations and enhancing quality, efficiency, and safety of care. By carefully examining and refining workflows, healthcare organizations can reduce errors, minimize delays, and improve overall quality of care. A well-optimized process ensures that resources are utilized effectively, leading to better clinical outcomes. Efficiency is the greatest driver of cost-containment. The emphasis on

Process Optimization requires a commitment to refining and enhancing operational processes. This ensures that health systems operate at the highest level of efficiency, maximizing productivity and minimizing waste.

Process optimization begins by thoroughly understanding existing procedures and identifying variations from recognized best practices to achieve desired outcomes. Within the health system, one of the hospitals had a goal to reduce post-operative complications. The most significant opportunity for improvement was the reduction of post-operative blood clots. Alongside mechanical and chemical blood clot prophylaxis, including physical therapy, routine ambulation emerged as a simple yet frequently overlooked intervention for preventing blood clots. Routine ambulation serves as an adjunct therapy in this context.

However, documentation of routine ambulation in patient records, especially outside of therapy sessions, was minimal. Furthermore, when patients were ambulated, there was no record of the frequency or distance, highlighting an area for improvement in tracking and enhancing patient care practices.

Six months after implementing daily 15-minute huddles where front-line team members report adherence to ambulation protocol for their patients, blood clot complications dropped by over 60%. The daily huddles were part of an initiative called "Managing for Daily Improvement" (MDI) led by the health systems performance improvement team.

In Element 4, Process Optimization, we discussed the considerable amount of waste and non-value-added work prevalent in many health-care organizations. To address this issue, BayCare Health System invested in a performance improvement team comprising mechanical engineers with Lean Six Sigma Black Belt certification. This strategic investment aimed to uncover inefficiencies and establish workflows that resulted in substantial cost savings, reaching hundreds of thousands of dollars, along with significant improvements in quality.

The Performance Improvement Team introduced Managing for Daily Improvement as a mechanism to establish process focused improvement around the nine Clinical Excellence measures and accelerate the journey to Top Quintile.

Managing for Daily Improvement is a powerful strategy to engage front line teams in performance improvement initiatives. It is particularly an effective method for changing behavior required to hardwire new processes. Every morning across BayCare's nursing units and ancillary departments, the team convened around the performance scorecard, forming a circle of collective commitment. At the center of their attention stood a visually striking scoreboard, resembling a traffic signal. Green symbolized successful adherence to the new process, while red signified a shortfall in compliance. The scoreboard was not just an ornament; it was a dynamic reflection of the team's resolve for change.

During the daily huddle, team members delved into a comprehensive review of the prior day's performance, updating the scoreboard with each hue representing progress or areas that needed attention. The scoreboard, once a mere visual aid, had evolved into an active participant in their relentless pursuit of improvement.

The potency of this visual management system lies in its ability to keep team members acutely aware of their progress. Green, embodying success, instilled pride and reinforced positive behaviors linked to the new process. Conversely, the red, signaling non-adherence, emerged as a compelling flag for change.

The daily reporting mechanism ensured that the process change remained a constant focal point. It created a continuous feedback loop, facilitating swift adjustments and corrections. Yet, it was not solely about the process; it was about the individuals comprising the team.

The visibility into individual team members' adherence to the new process became a formidable mechanism for behavior change. The prospect of reporting non-adherence during the daily huddle became a moment of vulnerability and potential embarrassment. The fear of seeing a red mark on the scoreboard transformed into a potent driver for accountability and personal responsibility.

With time, the daily huddles became a symbol of collective determination and a testament to the transformative power of visual management and daily reporting. The green and red hues on the scoreboard not only symbolized compliance with a new process but also narrated a tale of personal and collective growth. Each team member became a crucial contributor to the ongoing story of success.

As the daily huddles matured, the front-line teams learned to navigate the intersection of improvement and excellence, one green mark at a time, illuminating the path toward Clinical Excellence.

A Bedside to Boardroom Cadence of Accountability

Establishing and maintaining clinical excellence necessitates a consistent and structured approach to accountability. A Cadence of Accountability involves regular assessments, performance reviews, and an unwavering commitment to continuous improvement at all organizational levels. This rhythm of responsibility ensures healthcare organizations remain focused on goals, adapting to challenges and evolving to meet the ever-changing needs of patients and the healthcare landscape.

Early in the ascent to Clinical Excellence, the Chair of the Board Quality Committee posed a question that you will find later in the self-assessment of your knowledge of health system quality governance. He asked how I knew whether the front-line teams, their leaders, their directors, or even their executives were adhering to best practice processes designed to achieve the Clinical Excellence goal.

Although this crossed the line from governance to management, his question was not intended to dictate how I manage quality; it was to help me consider ways to ensure a cadence of accountability for results that started at the bedside and went up through the boardroom.

This cadence ensures that teams and leaders at every level understand their role in driving improvement and their accountability for achieving results. Coined by our esteemed chair, Eric Obeck, and reflected in a graphic shown in every quality meeting across the health system, the term 'Cadence of Accountability' became one of the most influential drivers of the journey to Top Quintile.

The Managing for Daily Improvement huddles were being developed on nursing units and ancillary departments across the health system's hospitals and ambulatory care divisions. The daily huddles, where frontline teams gathered to evaluate their adherence to processes aimed at enhancing Clinical Excellence measures, served as the foundational layer in the bedside-to-boardroom cadence of accountability.

At the onset of the pursuit of Clinical Excellence, I was apprehensive regarding the preparedness of the organization's leaders to embrace openness, transparency, and vulnerability. These qualities hold immense significance in hospital leadership, especially when communicating efforts to address quality issues to the health system's CEO and executive team. When leaders shy away from transparency and vulnerability, organizational silos may emerge, potentially leading to a missed chance to seek assistance from the CEO and Board in overcoming barriers.

Effective communication is paramount for fostering a culture of trust and continuous improvement. Transparent reporting allows leaders to share both successes and challenges openly, providing a comprehensive understanding of the organization's performance. Moreover, displaying vulnerability by acknowledging areas that require improvement creates an environment that encourages collaboration and innovation. Leaders who embrace transparency and vulnerability demonstrate authenticity, which is crucial for building trust among their team and with the higher-ups. This approach not only facilitates a more informed decision-making process but also promotes a culture of accountability and adaptability, leading to enhanced patient care and sustained organizational success.

As part of the tactical strategy for achieving Clinical Excellence, the health system hospitals established key clinical improvement opportunities on each nursing unit. While most units had more than two areas for improvement, focusing on too many dilutes leaders' and teams' ability to concentrate and dedicate time to improvement efforts. Once the primary opportunity was identified, evidence-based processes were implemented.

To facilitate progress, the Quality team collaborated with hospital leaders and clinical teams to identify variances from measurable best practice processes that acted as barriers to reliable, high-quality outcomes. The daily huddles, dedicated to reviewing adherence to best practice processes from the previous day, kept teams informed of their progress and served as a mechanism for bedside accountability.

While a mature Managing for Daily Improvement (MDI) structure typically involves front-line team members leading daily huddles, the novelty of the MDI process required Nursing unit managers to take on this role initially. They were tasked with leading the daily huddles, addressing obstacles to best practices, and escalating issues up the chain when necessary. These daily huddles, centered on reviewing the prior day's performance regarding key processes for improving care, offered visibility for front-line teams. This visibility enabled them to recognize how their unique skills contributed to improved patient outcomes and organizational success.

In more advanced MDI practices, as team members grow accustomed to the MDI process, senior leaders within the organization participate in spontaneous rounding. They approach any available team member and request an explanation of their performance on the MDI scoreboard. This accountability mechanism is designed for reinforcing the significance of clinical excellence for the front-line teams and drawing attention to their important contribution to the organization's success.

The next layer in the cadence of accountability was the hospital Quality Council Committee. The charters for the quality councils were standardized across all hospitals to ensure a focus on the top-quality improvement opportunity for each hospital, aligned with the health system's overarching goal of reaching the national top quintile. The front-line nursing unit and department leaders were scheduled to report their current outcomes and adherence to the improvement processes that came from their daily huddle scorecard.

It was important to include hospital physician representation on the hospital and ambulatory quality councils. This served not only to establish a committee where leaders reporting their unit performance felt adequately prepared but also to actively involve hospital physicians in the pathway to Clinical Excellence. Despite skepticism from some executive peers who doubted the possibility of physicians dedicating two hours a month to the committee, I developed an approach that proved highly effective.

I interviewed physicians in each hospital to identify individuals for council membership. By highlighting the selective nature of the process, a competitive atmosphere was fostered among the physicians and their peers. This strategy proved effective, leading to active participation by several physicians in the quality council of each hospital. Their on-going commitment demonstrated a prominent level of engagement in enhancing patient care to meet the goals of clinical excellence.

The interviews played a crucial role in ensuring that physician members understood their role on the committee. It was emphasized that the purpose was not intended to address their specific specialty but rather to seek their support in achieving the overarching goal of Clinical Excellence for all patients in the hospital. Nurse managers and ancillary department leaders were scheduled to routinely report their progress toward the established goals at the monthly Quality Council, where the committee members, including the hospital president would provide feedback and guidance on their improvement efforts. The presidents gleaned information from their hospital quality council that would equip them for report out at the next level in the Cadence of Accountability.

The next level in the Bedside to Boardroom Cadence of Accountability was the system level quality council. The system level quality council membership included the health system executive team, and the Chief Medical Officers from each hospital. A part of the Clinical Excellence strategy was ensuring that each of the health systems hospital presidents could speak to the opportunities and improvement efforts for their scope of responsibility and that each demonstrated commitment to the organization goals.

To help foster commitment and engagement, I decided to have the presidents responsible for reporting their performance at the system quality council meeting. This was not a popular decision at first and their attendance and availability varied.

During a regular monthly meeting with Tommy Inzina, the health system's CEO, he inquired about the support I needed from him to achieve our Clinical Excellence goal. I asked him for 2 hours of his time to attend the system quality council, emphasizing the importance of holding leaders accountable for addressing top-priority quality measure gaps. This involved ensuring effective action plans were in place to address improvement opportunities and elevate overall quality performance.

Without fail, he attended the council meetings, actively engaging and holding presenters, including hospital presidents, accountable for progress in enhancing outcomes. Mr. Inzina's consistent presence at these forums established a solid layer of accountability in the bedside to boardroom cadence.

I knew that reporting to the system-level quality council was vital for hospital presidents as it showcased their personal accountability to the goals and visible commitment to clinical excellence. By being accountable to the system executive team, they developed a sense of ownership and recognized the importance of being able to articulate the progress toward goals in their individual hospitals. The hospital quality team members noted a noticeable increase in president involvement in improvement efforts following their participation in reporting to the system-level quality council.

As we developed the structural and operational framework for the pursuit of Clinical Excellence, I worked closely with each hospital president to make sure they understood their hospital's top opportunities and were committed to their role in achieving the health systems goal of Clinical Excellence. Each president was included as a member of the Quality Council at their respective hospital, which helped prepare them for the system level quality council. Over time they grew to understand the quality measure definitions and process improvement methodology used in their hospital performance improvement efforts.

The next level in the Cadence of Accountability was the Board Quality Committee. The committee was chaired by a Board of Directors member and included board members and health system physicians. The objective of the Board Quality Committee was to assess and govern progress toward the organization goal of Clinical Excellence. The standardized agenda included updates on performance improvement projects relevant to elevating system level outcomes. A substantial portion of the meeting agenda was dedicated to performance in the nine measures of Clinical Excellence.

The top layer in the Bedside to Boardroom Cadence of Accountability is the Board of Directors. The Board met quarterly and were instrumental in developing the Quality strategic plan and goals. New Board members attended an orientation to the Clinical Excellence strategic goals and their role in the Cadence of Accountability. The genuine engagement and commitment of the Board of Directors to effectively govern the Quality program was vital to the organization Ascent to Excellence.

Having laid the groundwork for success through structural and operational enhancements across all divisions of the health system, we were on our way to Clinical Excellence going warp speed.

Celebrating a Successful Clinical Excellence Journey

Annually, BayCare Health System organized a Quality Sharing Day for the entire workforce and Board of Directors. The event takes place at the local convention center to accommodate the participation of several thousand health system team members. The primary objective of Quality Sharing Day was to provide leaders and team members with a platform to showcase their quality improvement projects, either through break-out sessions or feature presentations. These presentations celebrated projects from the previous year that had resulted in notable enhancements in clinical, operational, or financial outcomes.

Quality Sharing Day served as a venue to highlight work involving frontline staff, illustrating how team members were both encouraged and empowered to drive meaningful change. Although the Quality Sharing Day conference represented a significant investment for the health system, it was considered a high-value initiative in fostering engagement and maintaining a focus on health system's Quality Philosophy of continuous quality improvement.

At the annual Quality Sharing Day, approximately five years after the Board of Directors and Executive Team initiated discussions and strategic planning to achieve Clinical Excellence and the aspirational goal of reaching the national Top Quintile in quality, safety, and operational efficiency, I had the honor of delivering the Feature Presentation titled "Road to Top Quintile – A Clinical Excellence Journey." In this presentation, I highlighted the key elements that successfully propelled BayCare Health System from the bottom quartile to the national top quintile in overall health system performance compared to large health systems.

The transformation of BayCare Health System resulted from a combination of horizontal leadership alignment towards a shared goal and a vertical cadence of accountability. This framework established a matrix that accelerated progress and facilitated the achievement of goals. Leadership, ensuring data integrity, and optimizing processes to enhance outcomes are crucial components of performance improvement. Strengthening these elements within a framework of committed leadership and a structured cadence of accountability served as a roadmap to desired results and the achievement of Clinical Excellence.

A Harmonious Symphony of Success

Drawing on my experience in healthcare management and performance optimization, I worked with the BayCare Health System board and senior leadership team to develop a comprehensive tactical approach which resulted in significant and measurable improvements in quality outcomes, patient safety, patient satisfaction, and operational efficiency. Within four years, the health system made remarkable progress and surpassed the 80th percentile. By year five, which was the original timeline set by the board, the health system had climbed close to the 90th percentile in the nation.

Ascent to Excellence provides the essential elements that enable health system boards and leaders to identify root causes and implement effective improvement strategies. Whether focusing on a specific priority measure within a hospital or undertaking a comprehensive enterprise-wide improvement initiative, these elements form the foundation for achieving sustained high-quality, safe, and efficient care delivery.

The blueprint elements of Leadership Commitment, Data Integrity, Engaged Workforce, Process Optimization, and a Culture of Accountability create a harmonious symphony of success in healthcare. When these elements work together seamlessly, they elevate the quality of patient care, enhance operational efficiency, and position healthcare organizations as beacons of clinical excellence.

The Ascent to Excellence blueprint represents a holistic and synergistic approach to organizational excellence. The BayCare case study incorporating the five elements accelerated the organizations overall performance, reducing medical errors, improving patient satisfaction and maintained a consistent growth in the profit margin, which was mirrored in the health systems percentile improvement rankings. In addition to national recognition, the health system was one of few in the nation successful with upside revenue in the Centers for Medicare and Medicaid Services Hospital Value-Based Purchasing program.

By adopting this comprehensive formula, healthcare leaders can navigate the complexities of the industry, respond to challenges with agility, and provide the highest standard of care for their communities. In the pursuit of clinical excellence, this formula stands as a guide, empowering healthcare organizations to not only meet but exceed the expectations of patients and stakeholders alike.

APPENDIX

Culture Assessment for Executives and Senior Leadership

The Ascent to Excellence Assessment of Organization Culture

The following assessment measures the organization culture as related to the Elements of Ascent to Excellence. The Likert scale allows for a range of responses, from strongly disagree to strongly agree providing valuable insights into the perceived strength of the cultural elements in each area.

Evaluating the organizational culture of the health system necessitates considering the perspectives of individuals across all organizational levels. The Culture Assessment for Senior Leaders and Boards is designed for healthcare directors up to the Board level. The Culture Assessment for Managers and Teams is tailored for front-line or department managers and their respective teams.

Ensure fair representation across all levels in the Bedside to Boardroom Cadence of Accountability by ensuring an equal number of representatives complete the assessment. Scan the QR code to be directed to the "Ascent to Excellence Culture Assessment." Select the Cultural Assessment for

Senior Leadership and Board Members. Follow instructions to complete and submit the assessment. The results will be tabulated, and you will receive a summary assessment within 7 business days.

Leadership Commitment

These statements provide a comprehensive view of the organizational culture, leadership effectiveness, and strategic alignment within the health system. Participants can select the option that best reflects their perception of the organization's leadership commitment to quality improvement.

1. **The health system's Board members and/or leaders visibly demonstrate through behaviors and actions that people are the most important organizational asset.**

   [ ] 1 Strongly Disagree

   [ ] 2 Disagree

   [ ] 3 Neutral

   [ ] 4 Agree

   [ ] 5 Strongly Agree

2. **The Board of Directors are actively engaged in governing the quality of care as evidenced by thoughtful inquiry and holding the health system management teams accountable for results.**

   [ ] 1 Strongly Disagree

   [ ] 2 Disagree

   [ ] 3 Neutral

   [ ] 4 Agree

   [ ] 5 Strongly Agree

3. **Leaders at all levels of the health system can articulate the goals in the health system strategic plan.**

   [ ] 1 Strongly Disagree

   [ ] 2 Disagree

   [ ] 3 Neutral

   [ ] 4 Agree

   [ ] 5 Strongly Agree

4. **Health system leaders restrict the total number of goals in the strategic plan to ensure concentrated focus and adequate time for achieving results.**

   [ ] 1 Strongly Disagree

   [ ] 2 Disagree

   [ ] 3 Neutral

   [ ] 4 Agree

   [ ] 5 Strongly Agree

5. **Standards of Behavior are reflected in the organization's core values and embedded in employee evaluations.**

   [ ] 1 Strongly Disagree

   [ ] 2 Disagree

   [ ] 3 Neutral

   [ ] 4 Agree

   [ ] 5 Strongly Agree

6. **The health system Board members have the appropriate training, skills, and knowledge to govern healthcare quality, safety, and efficiency.**

   [ ] 1 Strongly Disagree

   [ ] 2 Disagree

   [ ] 3 Neutral

   [ ] 4 Agree

   [ ] 5 Strongly Agree

7. **Leaders at all levels of the health system have an opportunity to attend conferences, lectures, or other external means of leadership growth and development.**

   [ ] 1 Strongly Disagree

   [ ] 2 Disagree

   [ ] 3 Neutral

   [ ] 4 Agree

   [ ] 5 Strongly Agree

8. **Leaders in our organization prioritize and invest in technology and tools that facilitate quality improvement efforts.**

   [ ] 1 Strongly Disagree

   [ ] 2 Disagree

   [ ] 3 Neutral

   [ ] 4 Agree

   [ ] 5 Strongly Agree

9. **Our leadership actively supports and allocates resources for ongoing training and education in quality improvement methodologies.**

   [ ] 1 Strongly Disagree

   [ ] 2 Disagree

   [ ] 3 Neutral

   [ ] 4 Agree

   [ ] 5 Strongly Agree

10. **The health system's strategic plan incorporates balanced SMART (Specific, Measurable, Achievable, Relevant & Timely) measures across quality, workforce engagement, patient satisfaction, and financial performance.**

    [ ] 1 Strongly Disagree

    [ ] 2 Disagree

    [ ] 3 Neutral

    [ ] 4 Agree

    [ ] 5 Strongly Agree

Data Integrity

Leaders play a crucial role in ensuring that a health system has robust data analytic capabilities to support decision-making and improve overall performance. These questions can help leaders assess the current state of data analytic capabilities within the health system, identify areas for improvement, and ensure that data-driven decision-making is an integral part of the organizational culture.

1. **Leaders in our healthcare organization demonstrate a clear understanding of the significance of accurate and reliable data in quality improvement initiatives.**

   [ ] 1 Strongly Disagree

   [ ] 2 Disagree

   [ ] 3 Neutral

   [ ] 4 Agree

   [ ] 5 Strongly Agree

2. **Performance improvement efforts in our organization are strategically aligned with addressing the top drivers that hinder the achievement of desired goals.**

   [ ] 1 Strongly Disagree

   [ ] 2 Disagree

   [ ] 3 Neutral

   [ ] 4 Agree

   [ ] 5 Strongly Agree

3. **The executive leadership team can articulate the Clinical Documentation Improvement teams' impact on risk-adjustment in data, as well as clinical, operational, and financial KPIs.**

   [ ] 1 Strongly Disagree

   [ ] 2 Disagree

   [ ] 3 Neutral

   [ ] 4 Agree

   [ ] 5 Strongly Agree

4. **Leadership actively promotes and reinforces the importance of data accuracy and reliability among staff involved in quality improvement initiatives.**

   [ ] 1 Strongly Disagree

   [ ] 2 Disagree

   [ ] 3 Neutral

   [ ] 4 Agree

   [ ] 5 Strongly Agree

5. **Leadership recognizes the role of technology and analytic systems in maintaining data integrity and actively supports initiatives to improve data management infrastructure.**

   [ ] 1 Strongly Disagree

   [ ] 2 Disagree

   [ ] 3 Neutral

   [ ] 4 Agree

   [ ] 5 Strongly Agree

6. **Our Board members and leaders understand the importance of risk-adjusted data in assessing clinical outcomes.**

   [ ] 1 Strongly Disagree

   [ ] 2 Disagree

   [ ] 3 Neutral

   [ ] 4 Agree

   [ ] 5 Strongly Agree

7. **Scorecards based on unit or department level performance are maintained and shared routinely with front line employees.**

   [ ] 1 Strongly Disagree

   [ ] 2 Disagree

   [ ] 3 Neutral

   [ ] 4 Agree

   [ ] 5 Strongly Agree

8. **The health system leaders use external benchmarks to gauge performance and establish goals for improvement.**

   [ ] 1 Strongly Disagree

   [ ] 2 Disagree

   [ ] 3 Neutral

   [ ] 4 Agree

   [ ] 5 Strongly Agree

9. **The health system effectively utilizes data to identify areas for improvement in clinical outcomes and operational efficiency.**

   [ ] 1 Strongly Disagree

   [ ] 2 Disagree

   [ ] 3 Neutral

   [ ] 4 Agree

   [ ] 5 Strongly Agree

10. **Senior leaders ensure that goals established in their departments directly or indirectly impact the organization goals in the health system strategic plan.**

    [ ] 1 Strongly Disagree

    [ ] 2 Disagree

    [ ] 3 Neutral

    [ ] 4 Agree

    [ ] 5 Strongly Agree

Engagement

Participants can respond to each statement based on their perceptions of the importance of employee engagement in the context of high-performing health systems and strong leadership.

1. **The hospital or health system performs at least one employee engagement survey per year.**

   [ ] 1 Strongly Disagree

   [ ] 2 Disagree

   [ ] 3 Neutral

   [ ] 4 Agree

   [ ] 5 Strongly Agree

2. **The hospital or health system leaders I work with exemplify behaviors of caring, compassion and respect.**

   [ ] 1 Strongly Disagree

   [ ] 2 Disagree

   [ ] 3 Neutral

   [ ] 4 Agree

   [ ] 5 Strongly Agree

3. **When faced with competing work priorities, I always choose to focus on what puts patients or our people first.**

   [ ] 1 Strongly Disagree

   [ ] 2 Disagree

   [ ] 3 Neutral

   [ ] 4 Agree

   [ ] 5 Strongly Agree

4. **Leadership consistently communicates a compelling vision and organization performance to goals that fosters employee commitment and enthusiasm.**

   [ ] 1 Strongly Disagree

   [ ] 2 Disagree

   [ ] 3 Neutral

   [ ] 4 Agree

   [ ] 5 Strongly Agree

5. **Leaders and team members are monetarily incentivized through a bonus structure to strive for goal achievement in quality & safety.**

   [ ] 1 Strongly Disagree

   [ ] 2 Disagree

   [ ] 3 Neutral

   [ ] 4 Agree

   [ ] 5 Strongly Agree

6. **Employee engagement is a dedicated objective in the health system's strategic goal.**

   [ ] 1 Strongly Disagree

   [ ] 2 Disagree

   [ ] 3 Neutral

   [ ] 4 Agree

   [ ] 5 Strongly Agree

7. **The health system's leadership actively promotes a positive and inclusive work culture.**

   [ ] 1 Strongly Disagree

   [ ] 2 Disagree

   [ ] 3 Neutral

   [ ] 4 Agree

   [ ] 5 Strongly Agree

8. **Leadership demonstrates transparency and openness in communication with employees.**

   [ ] 1 Strongly Disagree

   [ ] 2 Disagree

   [ ] 3 Neutral

   [ ] 4 Agree

   [ ] 5 Strongly Agree

9. **The health system recognizes and celebrates loyalty and years of service by sponsoring events dedicated to employees, including off-site award banquets.**

   [ ] 1 Strongly Disagree

   [ ] 2 Disagree

   [ ] 3 Neutral

   [ ] 4 Agree

   [ ] 5 Strongly Agree

10. **Our Board of Directors effectively govern our hospital or health systems quality program, ensuring progress toward desired outcomes.**

   [ ] 1 Strongly Disagree

   [ ] 2 Disagree

   [ ] 3 Neutral

   [ ] 4 Agree

   [ ] 5 Strongly Agree

Process Optimization

Assessing the focus on process improvement to drive clinical outcomes is crucial for ensuring a health system's commitment to delivering high-quality care. The following assessment questions can help evaluate the organization's approach to process improvement in the context of clinical outcomes:

1. **The health system has a performance improvement team of engineers with expertise in optimizing workflow processes and systems.**

   [ ] 1 Strongly Disagree

   [ ] 2 Disagree

   [ ] 3 Neutral

   [ ] 4 Agree

   [ ] 5 Strongly Agree

2. **The health system has a performance improvement team with individual performance improvement or Lean certifications with expertise optimizing workflow processes and systems.**

   [ ] 1 Strongly Disagree

   [ ] 2 Disagree

   [ ] 3 Neutral

   [ ] 4 Agree

   [ ] 5 Strongly Agree

3. **Leadership in our health system demonstrates a clear understanding of the distinction between outcome measures and process measures.**

   [ ] 1 Strongly Disagree

   [ ] 2 Disagree

   [ ] 3 Neutral

   [ ] 4 Agree

   [ ] 5 Strongly Agree

4. **Leadership prioritizes the establishment and tracking of key process measures to enhance overall performance.**

   [ ] 1 Strongly Disagree

   [ ] 2 Disagree

   [ ] 3 Neutral

   [ ] 4 Agree

   [ ] 5 Strongly Agree

5. **The health system's leaders ensure that outcome measures and strategic goals are aligned and patient-centric.**

   [ ] 1 Strongly Disagree

   [ ] 2 Disagree

   [ ] 3 Neutral

   [ ] 4 Agree

   [ ] 5 Strongly Agree

6. **There is a systematic approach to identifying and eliminating inefficiencies in our health system's processes.**

   [ ] 1 Strongly Disagree

   [ ] 2 Disagree

   [ ] 3 Neutral

   [ ] 4 Agree

   [ ] 5 Strongly Agree

7. **Staff across various departments are actively engaged in continuous improvement efforts driven by the health system's process engineering capabilities.**

   [ ] 1 Strongly Disagree

   [ ] 2 Disagree

   [ ] 3 Neutral

   [ ] 4 Agree

   [ ] 5 Strongly Agree

8. **There are dedicated efforts to identify and eliminate non-value-added work while implementing streamlined processes throughout the organization.**

   [ ] 1 Strongly Disagree

   [ ] 2 Disagree

   [ ] 3 Neutral

   [ ] 4 Agree

   [ ] 5 Strongly Agree

9. **Board members and/or senior executives ensure a process focused approach to performance improvement.**

   [ ] 1 Strongly Disagree

   [ ] 2 Disagree

   [ ] 3 Neutral

   [ ] 4 Agree

   [ ] 5 Strongly Agree

10. **The health system hospitals conduct Managing for Daily Improvement huddles to manage the process improvements for data driven top opportunities.**

    [ ] 1 Strongly Disagree

    [ ] 2 Disagree

    [ ] 3 Neutral

    [ ] 4 Agree

    [ ] 5 Strongly Agree

Accountability

A health system culture of accountability is foundational for delivering high-quality, safe, and efficient healthcare, fostering continuous improvement, and building trust among stakeholders. It contributes to the overall success and sustainability of the health system. The following questions assess the perception of the organization's culture of accountability.

1. **There is a clear and effective communication flow from front-line teams to senior leadership regarding progress and challenges.**

   [ ] 1 Strongly Disagree

   [ ] 2 Disagree

   [ ] 3 Neutral

   [ ] 4 Agree

   [ ] 5 Strongly Agree

2. **Nursing unit managers and ancillary leaders consistently address barriers to best practices during daily huddles.**

   [ ] 1 Strongly Disagree

   [ ] 2 Disagree

   [ ] 3 Neutral

   [ ] 4 Agree

   [ ] 5 Strongly Agree

3. **The hospital leadership demonstrates a commitment to promptly escalating issues up the chain of command when necessary.**

   [ ] 1 Strongly Disagree

   [ ] 2 Disagree

   [ ] 3 Neutral

   [ ] 4 Agree

   [ ] 5 Strongly Agree

4. **Hospital presidents transparently report progress toward quality and safety goals.**

   [ ] 1 Strongly Disagree

   [ ] 2 Disagree

   [ ] 3 Neutral

   [ ] 4 Agree

   [ ] 5 Strongly Agree

5. **Senior leaders regularly engage in spontaneous rounding, reviewing team scoreboards to ensure accountability.**

   [ ] 1 Strongly Disagree

   [ ] 2 Disagree

   [ ] 3 Neutral

   [ ] 4 Agree

   [ ] 5 Strongly Agree

6. **There is an effective bedside to boardroom cadence of accountability for goal achievement in my organization.**

   [ ] 1 Strongly Disagree

   [ ] 2 Disagree

   [ ] 3 Neutral

   [ ] 4 Agree

   [ ] 5 Strongly Agree

7. **Front-line teams have a clear understanding of their unique contribution to patient outcomes and organizational success.**

   [ ] 1 Strongly Disagree

   [ ] 2 Disagree

   [ ] 3 Neutral

   [ ] 4 Agree

   [ ] 5 Strongly Agree

8. **The health system leadership consistently emphasizes the importance of accountability in achieving clinical excellence goals.**

   [ ] 1 Strongly Disagree

   [ ] 2 Disagree

   [ ] 3 Neutral

   [ ] 4 Agree

   [ ] 5 Strongly Agree

9. **The health system boards and leaders prioritize a culture of accountability in their decision-making processes.**

   [ ] 1 Strongly Disagree

   [ ] 2 Disagree

   [ ] 3 Neutral

   [ ] 4 Agree

   [ ] 5 Strongly Agree

10. **The Hospital or health system CEO would know who to contact if the hospital value-based purchasing penalty was due to overutilization of Skilled Nursing Facilities.**

    [ ] 1 Strongly Disagree

    [ ] 2 Disagree

    [ ] 3 Neutral

    [ ] 4 Agree

    [ ] 5 Strongly Agree

Culture Assessment for Managers and Staff Members

The Ascent to Excellence Assessment of Organization Culture

The following assessment measures the organization culture as related to the Elements of Ascent to Excellence. The Likert scale allows for a range of responses, from strongly disagree to strongly agree providing valuable insights into the perceived strength of the cultural elements in each area.

Evaluating the organizational culture of the health system necessitates considering the perspectives of individuals across all organizational levels. The Culture Assessment for Senior Leaders and Boards is designed for healthcare directors up to the Board level. The Culture Assessment for Managers and Teams is tailored for front-line or department managers and their respective teams.

Ensure fair representation across all levels in the Bedside to Boardroom Cadence of Accountability by ensuring an equal number of representatives complete the assessment. Scan the QR code to be directed to the "Ascent to Excellence Culture Assessment." Select the Cultural Assessment for Managers and Teams. Follow instructions to complete and submit the assessment. The results will be tabulated, and you will receive a summary assessment within 7 business days.

Leadership Commitment

These statements provide a comprehensive view of the organizational culture, leadership effectiveness, and strategic alignment within the health system. Participants can select the option that best reflects their perception of the organization's leadership commitment to quality improvement.

1. **My leader consistently emphasizes the importance of delivering high-quality results in our work.**

   [ ] 1 Strongly Disagree

   [ ] 2 Disagree

   [ ] 3 Neutral

   [ ] 4 Agree

   [ ] 5 Strongly Agree

2. **My leader is committed to achieving and maintaining excellence in the outcomes of our projects and tasks.**

   [ ] 1 Strongly Disagree

   [ ] 2 Disagree

   [ ] 3 Neutral

   [ ] 4 Agree

   [ ] 5 Strongly Agree

3. **My leader actively supports and encourages efforts to improve the quality of our work.**

   [ ] 1 Strongly Disagree

   [ ] 2 Disagree

   [ ] 3 Neutral

   [ ] 4 Agree

   [ ] 5 Strongly Agree

4. **I feel confident that my leader takes necessary steps to ensure that our team's work meets or exceeds quality standards.**

   [ ] 1 Strongly Disagree

   [ ] 2 Disagree

   [ ] 3 Neutral

   [ ] 4 Agree

   [ ] 5 Strongly Agree

5. **My leader provides constructive feedback and guidance to help us enhance the quality of our outcomes.**

   [ ] 1 Strongly Disagree

   [ ] 2 Disagree

   [ ] 3 Neutral

   [ ] 4 Agree

   [ ] 5 Strongly Agree

6. **I perceive that my leader prioritizes the quality of our work over speed or quantity.**

   [ ] 1 Strongly Disagree

   [ ] 2 Disagree

   [ ] 3 Neutral

   [ ] 4 Agree

   [ ] 5 Strongly Agree

7. **My leader demonstrates a strong commitment to continuous improvement in the quality of our team's deliverables.**

   [ ] 1 Strongly Disagree

   [ ] 2 Disagree

   [ ] 3 Neutral

   [ ] 4 Agree

   [ ] 5 Strongly Agree

8. **I am confident that my leader values and recognizes the importance of quality in our daily tasks and projects.**

   [ ] 1 Strongly Disagree

   [ ] 2 Disagree

   [ ] 3 Neutral

   [ ] 4 Agree

   [ ] 5 Strongly Agree

9. **My leader actively seeks and implements strategies to enhance the overall quality of our team's performance.**

   [ ] 1 Strongly Disagree

   [ ] 2 Disagree

   [ ] 3 Neutral

   [ ] 4 Agree

   [ ] 5 Strongly Agree

10. **Quality assessment and performance improvement is a part of our annual required learning.**

    [ ] 1 Strongly Disagree

    [ ] 2 Disagree

    [ ] 3 Neutral

    [ ] 4 Agree

    [ ] 5 Strongly Agree

Data Integrity

Leaders play a crucial role in ensuring that a health system has robust data analytic capabilities to support decision-making and improve overall performance. These questions can help leaders assess the current state of data analytic capabilities within the health system, identify areas for improvement, and ensure that data-driven decision-making is an integral part of the organizational culture.

1. **Based on data shared with me, I know the top opportunity for quality improvement in my work area.**

   [ ] 1 Strongly Disagree

   [ ] 2 Disagree

   [ ] 3 Neutral

   [ ] 4 Agree

   [ ] 5 Strongly Agree

2. **I can state the overall strategic goals of the hospital and/or health system.**

   [ ] 1 Strongly Disagree

   [ ] 2 Disagree

   [ ] 3 Neutral

   [ ] 4 Agree

   [ ] 5 Strongly Agree

3. **I know how my contribution impacts the strategic goals of the hospital and/or health system.**

   [ ] 1 Strongly Disagree

   [ ] 2 Disagree

   [ ] 3 Neutral

   [ ] 4 Agree

   [ ] 5 Strongly Agree

4. **Leadership proactively advocates for enhancements to the Electronic Medical Record (EMR) system, aiming to improve documentation accuracy while minimizing unnecessary or duplicate entries.**

   [ ] 1 Strongly Disagree

   [ ] 2 Disagree

   [ ] 3 Neutral

   [ ] 4 Agree

   [ ] 5 Strongly Agree

5. **Scorecards based on unit or department level performance are maintained with the most current performance data and shared routinely with front line employees.**

   [ ] 1 Strongly Disagree

   [ ] 2 Disagree

   [ ] 3 Neutral

   [ ] 4 Agree

   [ ] 5 Strongly Agree

6. **The hospital and/or health system performance scorecards are easy to understand and gauge how the hospital and/or system is performing compared to goals.**

   [ ] 1 Strongly Disagree

   [ ] 2 Disagree

   [ ] 3 Neutral

   [ ] 4 Agree

   [ ] 5 Strongly Agree

7. **Our unit/department is held accountable to strict guidelines of accurate and timely documentation.**

   [ ] 1 Strongly Disagree

   [ ] 2 Disagree

   [ ] 3 Neutral

   [ ] 4 Agree

   [ ] 5 Strongly Agree

8. **I am aware that our Unit or department goals directly or indirectly impact the organization goals in the health system or hospital strategic plan.**

   [ ] 1 Strongly Disagree

   [ ] 2 Disagree

   [ ] 3 Neutral

   [ ] 4 Agree

   [ ] 5 Strongly Agree

9. **Daily huddles on our unit are valuable in identifying and resolving potential threats to high quality care.**

   [ ] 1 Strongly Disagree

   [ ] 2 Disagree

   [ ] 3 Neutral

   [ ] 4 Agree

   [ ] 5 Strongly Agree

10. **We have a unit performance scorecard visible to staff, patients and guests that is kept up to date and provides current progress to goals.**

    [ ] 1 Strongly Disagree

    [ ] 2 Disagree

    [ ] 3 Neutral

    [ ] 4 Agree

    [ ] 5 Strongly Agree

Engagement

Engaged employees contribute to a positive work culture, enhanced teamwork, and improved patient outcomes. Recognizing the importance of employee engagement, healthcare organizations strive to create environments that foster collaboration, communication, and a sense of purpose, leading to higher job satisfaction and better overall performance in delivering quality healthcare services. These statements cover key aspects of engagement, providing a comprehensive view of manager and team perceptions and experiences within the health system.

1. **The hospital or health system performs at least one employee engagement survey per year.**

   [ ] 1 Strongly Disagree

   [ ] 2 Disagree

   [ ] 3 Neutral

   [ ] 4 Agree

   [ ] 5 Strongly Agree

2. **I feel respected and trusted by the leaders and physicians I work with.**

   [ ] 1 Strongly Disagree

   [ ] 2 Disagree

   [ ] 3 Neutral

   [ ] 4 Agree

   [ ] 5 Strongly Agree

3. **I feel a keen sense of connection to the mission of our health system and/or hospital and am proud to work here.**

   [ ] 1 Strongly Disagree

   [ ] 2 Disagree

   [ ] 3 Neutral

   [ ] 4 Agree

   [ ] 5 Strongly Agree

4. **My direct supervisor consistently communicates a compelling vision and organization performance to goals that fosters employee commitment and enthusiasm.**

   [ ] 1 Strongly Disagree

   [ ] 2 Disagree

   [ ] 3 Neutral

   [ ] 4 Agree

   [ ] 5 Strongly Agree

5. **It would take more than higher pay or better benefits for me to leave my current employer.**

   [ ] 1 Strongly Disagree

   [ ] 2 Disagree

   [ ] 3 Neutral

   [ ] 4 Agree

   [ ] 5 Strongly Agree

6. **My leader holds our team accountable for adherence to behavior standards.**

   [ ] 1 Strongly Disagree

   [ ] 2 Disagree

   [ ] 3 Neutral

   [ ] 4 Agree

   [ ] 5 Strongly Agree

7. **The health system's leadership actively promotes a positive, diverse, and inclusive work culture.**

   [ ] 1 Strongly Disagree

   [ ] 2 Disagree

   [ ] 3 Neutral

   [ ] 4 Agree

   [ ] 5 Strongly Agree

8. **The top leaders in our hospital or health system demonstrate transparency and openness in communication with employees.**

   [ ] 1 Strongly Disagree

   [ ] 2 Disagree

   [ ] 3 Neutral

   [ ] 4 Agree

   [ ] 5 Strongly Agree

9. **The rewards and recognition program at my health system and/or hospital is effective and makes a positive difference in my level of engagement.**

   [ ] 1 Strongly Disagree

   [ ] 2 Disagree

   [ ] 3 Neutral

   [ ] 4 Agree

   [ ] 5 Strongly Agree

10. **Overall, employee engagement is one of the most important goals to leaders of my health system and/or hospital.**

    [ ] 1 Strongly Disagree

    [ ] 2 Disagree

    [ ] 3 Neutral

    [ ] 4 Agree

    [ ] 5 Strongly Agree

Process Optimization

The following statements reflect employee perceptions of process improvement within a healthcare setting. They cover various aspects related to commitment to the organization's mission, awareness and involvement in process changes, leadership priorities, efficiency in daily work, openness to change, training opportunities, and the focus on improving patient outcomes. The statements assess how employees perceive and engage with process improvement initiatives.

1. **My unit or department performance goals reflect our commitment to the health system and/or hospital mission and/or vision statement(s).**

   [ ] 1 Strongly Disagree

   [ ] 2 Disagree

   [ ] 3 Neutral

   [ ] 4 Agree

   [ ] 5 Strongly Agree

2. **Changes in processes that impact patient care rarely occur without my knowledge or involvement.**

   [ ] 1 Strongly Disagree

   [ ] 2 Disagree

   [ ] 3 Neutral

   [ ] 4 Agree

   [ ] 5 Strongly Agree

3. **The priority of my health system and/or hospital is excellent patient care.**

   [ ] 1 Strongly Disagree

   [ ] 2 Disagree

   [ ] 3 Neutral

   [ ] 4 Agree

   [ ] 5 Strongly Agree

4. **Leadership prioritizes the establishment and tracking of key process measures, (for example, ambulation frequency, timely antibiotic administration, or days in accounts receivable) to enhance overall outcomes.**

   [ ] 1 Strongly Disagree

   [ ] 2 Disagree

   [ ] 3 Neutral

   [ ] 4 Agree

   [ ] 5 Strongly Agree

5. **The hospital or health system's leaders ensure that outcome measures and strategic goals are aligned and patient-centric.**

   [ ] 1 Strongly Disagree

   [ ] 2 Disagree

   [ ] 3 Neutral

   [ ] 4 Agree

   [ ] 5 Strongly Agree

6. **Our daily work is very organized, without unnecessary time-wasting tasks.**

   [ ] 1 Strongly Disagree

   [ ] 2 Disagree

   [ ] 3 Neutral

   [ ] 4 Agree

   [ ] 5 Strongly Agree

7. **I always embrace change when I know it will result in better outcomes for our patients.**

   [ ] 1 Strongly Disagree

   [ ] 2 Disagree

   [ ] 3 Neutral

   [ ] 4 Agree

   [ ] 5 Strongly Agree

8. **I have never been asked to perform audits on patient charts for longer than a couple of weeks.**

   [ ] 1 Strongly Disagree

   [ ] 2 Disagree

   [ ] 3 Neutral

   [ ] 4 Agree

   [ ] 5 Strongly Agree

9. **My hospital or health system provides valuable training on quality of care and process improvement.**

   [ ] 1 Strongly Disagree

   [ ] 2 Disagree

   [ ] 3 Neutral

   [ ] 4 Agree

   [ ] 5 Strongly Agree

10. **Our unit or department focuses on changes or enhancement to existing processes to improve patient outcomes.**

    [ ] 1 Strongly Disagree

    [ ] 2 Disagree

    [ ] 3 Neutral

    [ ] 4 Agree

    [ ] 5 Strongly Agree

Accountability

A culture of accountability within the health system serves as the cornerstone for providing healthcare that is of high quality, safe, and efficient. It supports ongoing improvement efforts and helps establish trust among leaders and teams. This culture is integral to the overall success and long-term sustainability of the health system. The following statements aim to gauge the perceptions of both managers and staff members regarding accountability within their work areas.

1. **Sometimes I feel personal accountability for the care provided on my unit even when I am not there.**

   [ ] 1 Strongly Disagree

   [ ] 2 Disagree

   [ ] 3 Neutral

   [ ] 4 Agree

   [ ] 5 Strongly Agree

2. **In my unit or department, poor performance or behaviors that are not aligned with behavior standards are not tolerated.**

   [ ] 1 Strongly Disagree

   [ ] 2 Disagree

   [ ] 3 Neutral

   [ ] 4 Agree

   [ ] 5 Strongly Agree

3. **Team members in my unit take responsibility for their tasks and always help others to ensure patients receive the highest quality of care.**

   [ ] 1 Strongly Disagree

   [ ] 2 Disagree

   [ ] 3 Neutral

   [ ] 4 Agree

   [ ] 5 Strongly Agree

4. **Accountability for quality, safety and timely care delivery is emphasized and valued in the culture of my unit or department.**

   [ ] 1 Strongly Disagree

   [ ] 2 Disagree

   [ ] 3 Neutral

   [ ] 4 Agree

   [ ] 5 Strongly Agree

5. **There are clear expectations regarding accountability for performance within our team.**

   [ ] 1 Strongly Disagree

   [ ] 2 Disagree

   [ ] 3 Neutral

   [ ] 4 Agree

   [ ] 5 Strongly Agree

6. **I feel accountable for meeting deadlines and goals in my unit/department.**

   [ ] 1 Strongly Disagree

   [ ] 2 Disagree

   [ ] 3 Neutral

   [ ] 4 Agree

   [ ] 5 Strongly Agree

7. **There is a shared commitment among my team to achieve our unit or department objectives.**

   [ ] 1 Strongly Disagree

   [ ] 2 Disagree

   [ ] 3 Neutral

   [ ] 4 Agree

   [ ] 5 Strongly Agree

8. **There is great teamwork and clear expectations of our team and it's immediately obvious when a team member is not pulling their weight.**

   [ ] 1 Strongly Disagree

   [ ] 2 Disagree

   [ ] 3 Neutral

   [ ] 4 Agree

   [ ] 5 Strongly Agree

9. **Accountability for mistakes is managed constructively in my unit, promoting a culture of trust and caring.**

   [ ] 1 Strongly Disagree

   [ ] 2 Disagree

   [ ] 3 Neutral

   [ ] 4 Agree

   [ ] 5 Strongly Agree

10. **Accountability combined with compassion, trust and respect is a positive attribute in a hospital or health system.**

   [ ] 1 Strongly Disagree

   [ ] 2 Disagree

   [ ] 3 Neutral

   [ ] 4 Agree

   [ ] 5 Strongly Agree

ACKNOWLEDGEMENTS

I am blessed to have begun my leadership career with a hospital where the president truly embodied the organizations core values of care, competence, and trustworthiness. Dr. Roy Chew fostered accountability among leaders and demonstrated compassionate leadership, prioritizing people, quality of care, and organizational excellence. I extend my heartfelt thanks to Dr. Chew for his patience, guidance, and outstanding leadership. The invaluable lessons I gained from him continue to influence my leadership approach today, and I am eternally grateful.

I remember my first day as an interim hospital Chief Quality Officer (CQO). I was the hospital's quality director for a couple of years and was asked to fill the role on the executive team until a new CQO could be hired. Within minutes of sitting down at my desk, I was notified that the survey team was there for the hospital's tri-annual accreditation survey. Accreditation and Regulatory Compliance fell under the responsibility of the Chief Quality Officer. After a minute of panic, the Chief Nursing Officer, Dr. Brenda Kuhn was at my door, reassuring me that she'd be right by my side throughout the survey. From that pivotal moment onward, Brenda has been more than a colleague—she has been a steadfast mentor, providing constant encouragement, support, and friendship. Her guidance has played a pivotal role in my growth as a leader and as an individual. Brenda is a role model in nursing leadership and a passionate advocate for the profound and sacred work of healthcare. I owe much of my development and success to her invaluable influence and am profoundly grateful for the impact she has had on my professional and personal life.

I want to express my sincere gratitude to Dr. Bruce Flareau for entrusting a nurse executive from Ohio with the responsibility of spearheading a significant transformation in quality, safety, and clinical effectiveness within a large health system. Dr. Flareau's exceptional leadership skills and commitment to quality care created an environment conducive to fostering clinical excellence across BayCare Health System. As a thought leader and outstanding teacher and coach, he played a central role in leading one of the most successful Accountable Care Organizations in the nation. Dr. Flareau's guidance and unwavering support were instrumental in helping me maintain resilience as we navigated the Clinical Excellence journey together, ultimately exceeding national Top Quintile performance. His leadership has left an indelible mark, and I am truly appreciative for the invaluable lessons and opportunities for growth he provided throughout our collaborative efforts.

The key catalyst for rapidly advancing a health system's strategic objectives lies in the active involvement of a committed board of directors, especially when led by an outstanding board chair.

The acceleration of BayCare Health System's ascent to Clinical Excellence owes much to the dedication of Gay Lancaster, who led the BayCare Quality Committee of the Board, and Eric Obeck, at the helm of the Board of Directors. Their unwavering commitment played an indispensable role, making it possible for us to achieve significant milestones at an accelerated pace. I extend sincere appreciation to these two outstanding leaders for their steadfast dedication to providing the highest quality of care for the patients served across the BayCare Health System communities. The high standards they set for our executive leadership team propelled us to remarkable achievements. If every health system board of directors shared their determination, leadership acumen, and commitment to high-quality care, every health system in the nation would undoubtedly deliver exceptional results.

Initially, I hesitated to embark on writing a book about performance improvement, as my early successes in driving health system improvement only scratched the surface of my knowledge. The true depth came from an exceptional Performance Improvement team, comprised of Lean-certified, Six Sigma Black Belt engineers. I want to express my sincere thanks and deep appreciation to Sean Cancelliere, Eddie Perez, and Chhavi Gupta for teaching me the science of performance improvement.

Every individual within the Quality & Performance Improvement team at BayCare played a pivotal role in not just guiding leaders and team members in steering efforts toward strategic goals but also in showcasing remarkable patience, resilience, and a profound ability to propel improvement throughout a large, dynamic health system. I want to express my heartfelt gratitude to Dr. Paul Lewis, Cindy Righter, Linda Leon, Suzanne Chandler, Rebecca Tackitt and Teresa Galante, who were right by my side throughout the entire Clinical Excellence journey. Working closely with Dr. Lewis and these brilliant women was not only an honor but also a privilege. I learned so much from each of them. The collaboration with the remarkable BayCare Quality team made it the most exceptional experience I've ever had the privilege to be a part of.

An extra special thank you to my husband, Tim and my family, Blake, Katy, Joel, Alyssa, Chelsea, Kirk, Andrew & Allyn for your encouragement and loving support, with a special shout out to our youngest son Andrew, for introducing me to innovative technology, and encourages me to be open to new, exciting tools such as OpenAI for the use of ChatGPT which contributed to the research and refinement of the content in Ascent to Excellence – A Blueprint for Healthcare Board and Leadership Success.

ABOUT THE AUTHOR

Teri K. Sholder is founder and president of Sholder Healthcare Executive Consulting, LLC., specializing in transforming health system quality, safety and operational efficiency. As a seasoned clinical professional and certified professional coder, Teri offers practical insights on optimizing quality, safety, and operational efficiency within health systems. Her approach is both holistic and visionary, emphasizing the integration of cultural characteristics, evidence-based practices, and patient-centric care models to enhance the overall standard of healthcare delivery.

Beyond her written contributions, Teri's impact extends through speaking engagements and consulting services, where she collaborates with health system executive teams to implement transformative solutions. Teri's commitment to advancing healthcare quality has made her a sought-after consultant, resulting in significant improvements in patient outcomes and overall operational performance. "Ascent to Excellence" not only stands as a testament to Teri Sholder's expertise but also serves as a guiding beacon for healthcare professionals navigating the complexities of contemporary healthcare, with a steadfast focus on clinical excellence.

www.sholderhealth.org